George Thurber, Francis Brill

Farm-Gardening and Seed-Growing

George Thurber, Francis Brill

Farm-Gardening and Seed-Growing

ISBN/EAN: 9783337082864

Printed in Europe, USA, Canada, Australia, Japan

Cover: Foto ©Andreas Hilbeck / pixelio.de

More available books at **www.hansebooks.com**

FARM-GARDENING

AND

SEED-GROWING.

BY

FRANCIS BRILL,
OF THE MATTITUCK (L. I.) SEED FARM.

NEW AND ENLARGED EDITION.

WITH

SUGGESTIONS TO SEED-GROWERS.

BY

DR. GEORGE THURBER.

NEW YORK:
ORANGE JUDD COMPANY,
1902

Entered, according to Act of Congress, in the year 1883, by the
ORANGE JUDD COMPANY,
In the Office of the Librarian of Congress, at Washington.

PUBLISHERS' PREFACE.

Mr. Brill, in writing this work, made known for the first time, in this country at least, the methods followed by those who raise vegetable seeds as a business. Other works occasionally gave brief hints upon saving the few seeds required for the family garden, but by methods unsuited to operations on a commercial scale. The author is one of the few men well qualified to treat the subject practically.

The business of seed-growing is rapidly extending in this country, and is attended by a corresponding falling off of importations. It is an occupation that presents many inducements to the careful cultivator, not the least of which is the large returns per acre from land devoted to the crops. In the business of seed-growing, a reputation for strict integrity and intelligent care forms an important portion of the capital required. The name of the grower adds a money value to the product.

Market-farming is the growing of garden vegetables by farm culture. It is the form which our agriculture must assume as the country grows older and the population more dense. Farmers in the older States with high-priced lands can not afford to grow those crops which bring them in competition with cultivators of cheap lands in the newer States, and they must devote them to crops which can not be transported to a great distance and for which there is a constant local demand.

The two branches of agriculture, or more properly, of

horticulture—Seed-growing and Farm-gardening may often be properly united. This new edition presents valuable suggestions to the intelligent seed-grower.

It is a well-established fact that while seeds may be true to their kind and every care taken to insure purity and freedom from the seeds of weeds, the larger the individual seeds, the more valuable they are. Large size indicates that the seeds came from healthy, vigorous plants, and that they attained their fullest development. Direct experiment shows that large seeds produce larger and stronger seedlings than do small seeds of the same variety. It also shows that this superiority at the start is maintained throughout the growth of the plants and is manifest at the time of harvest.

While the seeds of some plants, which originally came from cool and moist climates, may be more readily grown in Europe than here, the number of these is small. A large share of our garden-vegetables are natives of subtropical or even tropical countries, and these in our warm soils and under our clear bright skies, attain a perfection unknown in Europe. They mature more thoroughly and produce larger and better seed than it is possible to raise abroad. As a consequence the former prejudice of our gardeners against American seeds has well-nigh disappeared; and at present not only are they preferred at home, but the quantities exported annually increase.

Farm-Gardening and Seed-Growing.

INTRODUCTION.

A few years since, while residing at Newark, N. J., and engaged in market-gardening and seed-growing, the idea of writing a book on the latter subject was suggested to me by one of the editors of the *American Agriculturist*.

I thought the matter over, and finally abandoned the idea, from the fact that I did not believe the subject contained matter enough for a separate volume. Since my removal to the eastern part of Long Island—a section, by the way, admirably adapted to the production of vegetables and seeds—and noticing the interest manifested here by the farmers in matters pertaining to gardening, I have concluded to write a book on the leading vegetables and their seeds.

The market-gardens about the larger cities, especially New York, are being, one by one, cut up for building purposes, to accommodate the mass of people whose occupations are in the city, but who are obliged to find a dwelling-place beyond its limits. Hence it would seem that the time will soon be when the consumer must depend upon the "farm-garden" of remote districts for a supply of vegetables of many kinds, and the finer sorts alone, which are not transportable, will be the principal articles grown near the city.

Even now there are many places where land can be bought for the amount of money paid annually for rent by many market-gardeners, where the soil is as well adapted, naturally, for growing many vegetable crops as any can be.

At the present low prices of produce and the unequal price of labor, farmers can no longer depend upon the usual crops, and are anxious to turn their ground to good account by growing root crops and other vegetables which may be transported to market from a distance, and to aid such in accomplishing this object is the mission of one part of this work.

The growing of seeds has become an important branch of farm industry, and the increasing demand for all leading seeds, owing to the constant growth of our country, and the accompanyingly increased interest in horticulture, render this business worthy the attention of those having land suitable for the purpose. Seed-raising may be conducted in connection with farm-gardening to good advantage, or carried on separately. If, perchance, some of my readers may be assisted, by means of the instructions given, to establish for themselves or their sons a business at once pleasant, healthful, and lucrative, the object of this work will have been attained.

In preparing the book, I have endeavored to give plain, practical directions, in minute detail, for growing vegetables and seeds, and have aimed to avoid all superfluous matter, which, though it might be interesting to the general reader, would be of no practical benefit to those for whom the work is more especially designed. I have deemed it advisable to dispense with illustrations, which I admit are useful, to a certain extent, in giving to the reader a more vivid idea of the form and general appearance of the subject under consideration; but in these days of enterprise, almost every seedsman's catalogue, as well as the works on gardening which have preceded this, and the agricultural and horticultural journals, contain complete illustrations of all leading vegetables, implements, etc. A repetition of them here would only increase the size of the volume without materially adding to its usefulness.

In giving directions for sowing, planting, etc., the dates are for the latitude of New York City, and should be varied according as the situation is north or south of that point.

MARKET-GARDENING.

This term as generally used applies to the growing of vegetables for market in so-called market-gardens. These are usually tracts of land lying adjacent to the larger cities, and comprise from five to fifteen acres. It is important that the market-gardener should be near to market for various reasons. His crops are mostly sold in the green state; many of them, being forced under glass, are consequently of a very perishable nature and are easily damaged by rough handling; hence by carting to market in wagons, and being handled only by himself, or those in his immediate employ, his produce is not subjected to such severe treatment as is often given to articles of freight by railroad or steamboat employés. Moreover, from the very perishable nature of many garden vegetables, they can not be long packed in bulk without heating, hence the quicker they are sold and consumed after gathering the better.

Another very important point is the facility for obtaining manure from the stables in the city, which by their system of planting must be used in immense quantities. There may be some readers of this book who, having land near large villages, where there is generally a good market, may desire to pay some attention to this business. To such I would say, the manner of sowing, cultivating, etc., is very similar to the directions herein given for the farm-garden.

For valuable information on market-gardening I would respectfully recommend to them "Gardening for Profit," a practical work, giving a full *exposé* of the system of that business as practised about New York City, and written by Peter Henderson, one of the most successful gardeners of that vicinity.

FARM-GARDENING.

This term may be applied to the growing of garden vegetables more remote from market. The farm-gardens of the present day are not very far distant from the cities, and in them are grown many vegetables which are found in the market-garden, but usually the main crops are the coarser articles best adapted to transportation, and such as do not require excessively heavy manuring. As I remarked in the Introduction, the time must come when the production of grain and all farm produce must be left to the great West, and all suitable land within a radius of at least one hundred miles of our present commercial centers will be occupied as farm-gardens in producing vegetables for the millions who will be engaged in mercantile and mechanical pursuits in the cities, fast spreading over the sections now used for the purpose of gardening. I have no desire to be prophetic, but if we may judge of the future by the past, this view would seem to be well founded. This work, so far as it treats on the growing of vegetables, is intended principally for those who now or may in the future have land distant from the great market centers who may desire to change their business.

While I have scrupulously avoided in every case writing anything in regard to the possible or probable amount of money to be realized from any crop, I must say that beyond a doubt there are many vegetable crops which may be grown far remote from, and shipped to market, that will pay much greater profits than ordinary farm produce.

What these crops shall be and the amount to be realized from them can only be determined by the attending circumstances. The class of men above alluded to, or, in other words, those who are now engaged in farming—working men—can enter upon this business at much less risk than those entirely unskilled in tilling the soil. They can, in connection with their regular business, devote an acre or two to growing those crops the management of which is the least complicated. The additional expense will be for manure, some improved tools, and a little extra labor. By keeping strict account of expenses and receipts, they can calculate nearly the probable amount of money return from each crop.

I would here call attention to the fact that a trial of three or four years will be necessary to fully determine this matter, because the land at the start can hardly be brought to the condition necessary to produce the best results, which can only be brought about by thorough working and manuring. It also may occur that at one season the price of any particular article may be very low, and the next exactly the reverse may be the case, so that one year's results must be averaged with the other. If these experiments prove satisfactory, the area devoted to the culture may be increased, and other crops, such as require the use of hot-beds and cold-frames, may be added.

Those who have sons growing up can assist them in this way to acquire a knowledge of this kind of farming, and as a rule, those who have grown up with the business are the most successful followers of it. In most cases, in farm-gardening, one half the quantity of manure used by market-gardeners will be sufficient to produce the crop, especially on new land that is naturally fertile, and where land is abundant it will be advisable to select a fresh piece occasionally—one that has lain for some time in grass—and seed down an equivalent amount of the old land. There are many crops which may be grown for

1*

an indefinite number of years on the same land, but as a rule, alternating or changing crops occasionally is advisable. It will be well to plant the new ground, for one or two years, with such crops as can be worked by plow and cultivator, the better to subdue it and prepare it for those which require hand cultivation.

Never sow nor plant more ground than can be positively sure to receive proper and timely attention, and bear in mind that to the gardener there is no season of rest; wet or dry, hot or cold, there will always be something to do, which must be done in its proper time to insure success.

SEED-GROWING.

This business is an extended branch of vegetable-growing, for the operations of growing the crop from which to produce the seed are the same as when raising it for market, except, perhaps, in many instances it is not essential to grow the *stock* so early, and in some cases, as with egg-plant, unusual attention is requisite in forwarding the plants, to get a season long enough in which to mature the seeds. The business of seed-growing, like farm gardening, can only be acquired by practice, and should not be entered upon very largely at the start. In addition to lack of experience, another serious drawback to the beginner in seed-growing, is the difficulty in procuring a market for the seeds when grown.

The seedsmen of the present day vie with each other in procuring and selling the most reliable seeds, for they understand full well the importance to the gardener of having only such as are fresh and pure, for should he sow any other his labor will have been in vain. I must here call the attention of those who contemplate farm-gardening or seed-growing, to the vast importance of obtaining and sowing only fresh and pure seeds; for should they fail to germinate, the ground will be lost for that crop at least, and when the stock is impure the case will be still more serious. For instance, if cabbage, lettuce, or any crop of this kind, upon which much labor has been expended, proves other than what it should be, the result must be damaging, if not ruinous. In view of these facts, seedsmen are very particular to buy only from known and responsible growers; hence, the new beginner must aim to establish a reputation for responsibility. In seed-growing, great care must be taken to keep far apart such as will mix by the blossom, and it is advisable not to grow seeds in many varieties of any one class of vegetable. It is further of great importance always to save "stock seed" from the very best of whatever kind, and in saving the main crop to select only perfect specimens.

In describing the varieties of the different kinds of vegetables, I have noticed only such as are the most popular about New York, and the descriptions are mainly to aid in making selections for seed. For a complete list of varieties and descriptions in minute detail of almost every known vegetable, the reader is referred to a book entitled "Vegetables of America," by Fearing Burr, Jr., the most complete work of its class ever published in this country.

SOIL AND PREPARATION.

The soil for growing vegetables and seeds should be as near as possible a deep loam; it may be more or less sandy, but avoid clay, or anything heavier than a clay loam. It should have a free but not too porous subsoil, and if not dry, should be made so by draining. Here I would say, if possible, select a soil that is naturally dry, or, in other words, that which will not retain the surface water.

It is quite as important that the subsoil be such as to

allow the moisture to ascend in dry weather, as to descend in wet weather, and while draining may assist the latter, it can never fully accomplish the former; hence, the preference for *natural* to *made* land. The preparations should be made, so far as possible, in the fall. The ground should be plowed, thoroughly harrowed, and smoothed off with the back of the harrow, where early planting is to be done, as the water passes away easier from an even surface, and the soil is sooner dry in the spring, but such land as is intended for later crops may be left without harrowing. Fallow ground should be taken for sowing seeds on, but sward land may be used for such crops as are to be worked with the cultivator, provided it can be plowed in August, and again plowed and thoroughly harrowed late in the fall. Land lying nearly level with a southern aspect is to be preferred. The beds may be laid out of any size, but should not be short, or too much time will be consumed in turning while plowing. A convenient size is ten yards wide and one hundred and twenty yards long, containing very nearly one quarter of an acre. A narrow headland should be left at each end, for driving on and for turning when plowing. If pains are taken to lay out the lands *straight* in the start, they may always be kept so with very little trouble.

MANURES AND MANURING.

Without fertilizers to enrich the soil, all attempts to grow vegetables or seeds will be in vain; in fact, liberal manuring and careful attention to growing crops are the two most essential points in the business.

Stable manure has always been considered the best, and is now the standard fertilizer with market-gardeners, although others are used to some extent. Farmers who have been in the habit of using from ten to twenty loads of coarse barn-yard manure to the acre, will be astonished when told that market-gardeners use four times the last-named amount, or more, of well-rotted stable manure, every year.

In fact, they put on as much as can be conveniently turned under, with the assistance of two men, following the plow and scraping it into the furrows. Of concentrated manures they apply more than double the quantity used for farm crops; of bone-dust one ton, Peruvian guano one half a ton to the acre, and so on.

This heavy manuring is necessary, as they plant very close, raise two crops a year, and take an immense amount of produce from the land.

In farm-gardening or seed-growing, where the crop is generally planted wide, and there is an abundance of land to allow of a portion being seeded down at times and allowed to rest, one half the above-named quantities of manure will suffice.

It is always advisable to use stable manure *mainly*, when it can be obtained, and in following the directions herein given for manuring the various crops, bear in mind that I always have reference to such as is obtained from cities, when speaking of stable-manure. This is nearly free from straw, and, load for load, is worth double such as is usually made in barn-yards, and composed largely of straw, stalks, etc. This city manure is bulky, and when freighted by railroad, as it is to a great extent on Long Island, the first cost is high, but I am fully satisfied that, to a certain extent, it is the cheapest in the end.

Next to this, *pure* ground bone, when applied in proper quantity, is preferable. This is very rich in fertilizing properties, and may be used on alternate years with stable manure to good advantage.

The soil for vegetable-growing requires to be mealy and free from lumps, and it can be kept so by means of the decaying vegetable matter contained in stable-manure.

But so far as fertilizing properties go, I am not sure but pure fine bone is much cheaper than coarse manure. In sections where *prime* stable-manure can not be obtained, I would advise liberal applications of bone in connection with green crops plowed under; the former as a fertilizer, and the latter to keep the soil in good working condition. Ground bone is now made of various grades, generally designated as bone-dust, bone-meal, and bone-flour. The former is the best for permanent crops, such as asparagus, rhubarb, etc., and for seeding down to grass for renewing the land; the second is suited to crops sown in the fall, such as spinach, etc., but in either case, unless the ground is sufficiently rich to give the plants a start, bone-flour or guano must be used, in connection with the bone dust or meal. Bone-flour is very fine, and acts quickly, nearly as much so as guano, and hence is preferable for crops which mature the same season they are sown or planted. There is much adulterated bone sold at the present day, and those who have used this kind have become discouraged, and say that bone is of no value.

There are, however, some conscientious men engaged in this business, and among them are Lister Brothers, of Newark, N. J. It may seem out of place here to insert anything that may seem like an advertisement, but as I always use the bone ground by the above firm, and from a long and intimate acquaintance with them, and frequent visits to their factory while I resided near it, I can recommend their productions as pure and reliable, and I deem it just to the patrons of this work to inform them where they can obtain a pure article in this line. There is one thing about bone which many do not seem to comprehend. Let it be never so fine it does not impart *all* its fertilizing properties at once, hence liberal applications must be made, and the most soluble parts will act on the present crop, while the balance will benefit the future ones.

Peruvian guano is a powerful fertilizer, but requires to be evenly distributed to prevent the growing plants from coming in contact with any considerable portion of it, as it is apt to be injurious to the young roots when they are brought in sudden contact with it.

Fish are used largely for manure at the eastern part of Long Island and along the coast generally, and make a valuable fertilizer. An excellent compost can be made by mixing muck and fish, one small load of the former to one thousand of the latter, and afterwards working the whole over with an equal bulk of stable manure. "Fish guano," that is, the "scraps," flesh, and bones of fish from which the oil has been extracted, is also a valuable fertilizer. Wood-ashes possess valuable fertilizing properties, and are very beneficial in preventing the ravages of worms which attack plants at the roots. There are few or none of the many compound manures which possess any real value for gardening purposes.

Green manures possess great fertilizing and renovating properties, and there is nothing better for land than a crop of clover plowed under. Buckwheat, corn, oats, etc., etc., may be used for this purpose to advantage, but clover is far the best, as the foliage not only enriches, but the roots permeate and loosen the soil.

It is always preferable to apply manures of whatever kind broadcast, but when this is not practicable, and "manuring in the hills" has to be resorted to, if stable manure is used, let it be well rotted, and when applied, thoroughly mixed with the soil, the better to retain moisture.

A mixture of fish or fish scrap, muck, and rotted manure, makes an excellent compost for manuring in the hill. The term "hill" as herein used should not be deemed to imply that the ground must be raised, which would be injurious, except in case of sweet-potatoes, watermelons, and such plants as require a very dry soil. The term is a very common one, and serves to distinguish between manuring broadcast, or at specified distances. Some spread the manure broadcast over the land in the fall and winter; this plan, however, is practised mainly by farmers, and is seldom resorted to by gardeners, who prefer to cart out the manure the latter part of winter, place it in large heaps near the point where it is to be used, and cart on the land and spread it, immediately before plowing.

SOWING SEEDS.

The proper distribution of seed in sowing is quite important, and there are few who can do it just right. Happily, machines have been invented for the purpose, and many of them do the work more evenly than it can possibly be done by hand. Some seeds, from their peculiar formation, have to be sown by hand. It is a very difficult matter to give directions for sowing seeds, and to say how much is required to the acre. Much depends upon the season, and also upon the freshness of the seed, and even seed known to be new may be partly deficient in germinating properties.

The best rule is, when sowing in rows, to be governed by the character of the seed and relative strength of the young plants—for instance, carrot, parsnip, and some others have light seed, and the young plants are feeble. Such should be sown thickly, and afterward be thinned out, as directed under each separate head.

Others—plants such as cucumbers, melons, etc.—are liable to be attacked by bugs, and it is well to make some allowance on this account. Most heavy seeds can be sown thin, especially if broadcast, the chances being that they will be too thick, especially if sown by inexperienced hands. Take, for instance, the seed of flat turnip, one pound of which, in measure but little more than a pint, will sow an acre of land, but it requires a very nice calculation to get the seed evenly distributed and make such a small quantity cover so much ground.

Seeds sown by machine may be regulated by sowing first on a cloth or floor, and setting the gauge to the proper grade. Some seeds are variable in size; such should be divided by sifting, and, if sown by machine, put in separately. It is advisable, if possible, to always sow as soon as the ground is prepared, while the surface soil is still fresh and moist, and when covered by raking, always draw the rake lengthwise with the rows. Very fine seed must not be covered too deep. Directions on this point are given under each separate head.

TRANSPLANTING.

This is a very important operation, and but few understand it properly. As a rule, a plant when set out should be so firmly fastened that upon taking the point of a leaf between the thumb and forefinger it will break away before the plant can be pulled out. Even this test may be withstood and the plant still die, from the fact that it is improperly planted. It is often the case that a mass of earth is pressed against the stalk at the surface, while the root is left so loose that it can not get established at once, and the plant dies, or lingers along until perchance there comes a rain to wash the earth about the root, when it starts feebly, and at maturity can not be what it might have been had not its growth been materially checked at the start. With the dibble make a hole larger than the root, that the fibers may be in a natural position; put in the plant to the first leaves, or as deep as possible without covering the heart. Holding the plant with the left hand, pass the point of the dibble down, *close to the plant*, carrying with it a little soil, which press firmly *against the root*, and knock loose soil into the hole left by the dibble.

Soil pressed against the *stalk* near the surface has a tendency to prevent the earth from washing down and settling about the root, and can not possibly be of any use.

The operation of transplanting should always be done, if in spring or autumn, while the earth is fresh, as planting in dry soil is very tedious, the holes filling as fast as made. For summer transplanting it is best to prepare and mark out the land in good season. When the rain comes, be ready to go at it while the soil is in condition, and unless the amount of rain is such as to make the earth thin mud, do not stop, for there may not soon be another chance. It sometimes may occur that the summer rains may not be sufficient to thoroughly saturate the soil and insure growth of the plants. In this case "puddling" must be resorted to. Near the plant-bed make a hole about one foot diameter, and six or eight inches deep; into this pour water, and with a hoe mix to the consistency of paste or thin mud, which will adhere to the roots. Let the plants be held evenly in the hands, and the roots passed a few times through the mud as each handful is pulled. Lay them in baskets, protect from the sun and air as much as possible, and have them transplanted very soon after they are pulled.

In taking up plants from the cold-frame, use a spade to raise them, thus securing whole roots with considerable earth attached. Plants in hot-beds should be saturated well with water before pulling, to accomplish the same object.

The work of transplanting may be greatly facilitated by adopting a regular system of operations. Let one man attend to pulling the plants after enough have been drawn for a start. Have an active boy for each man to carry and drop the plants. If desirable to have the plants at even distances in the rows, mark the same on a pole, and by it plant the middle one of every seven or nine rows, which answers as a guide for the boys, who can drop the plants on the other rows, either side, directly opposite. The top of the plant should be laid to the left hand of the planters, to be the more readily taken up for depositing in the hole, which, by the way, should be made with a dibble in the right hand while the plant is being picked up with the left.

It is not advisable to drop out plants of celery, leek, etc., which are set close in the rows, but here time may be saved by having one person to carry the plants in a basket, and hand them out as wanted by the planters. Should watering have to be resorted to, let it be done while there is no sun on the plants, as this would scorch the leaves, and the surface of the soil be apt to bake. The best time for watering is after sundown, or at least late in the afternoon.

In transplanting into cold-frame or hot-bed, let the earth be freshly dug or raked, and after setting the plants, partially shade them for a few days, but do not wholly exclude the light. Use two broad boards to step on; the face of one of these may be notched out at the distances required between the plants, when regularity is desired.

INSECTS.

The insects which annoy the gardener and damage or destroy his crops are of several kinds.

The Striped Bug is very destructive to young plants of cucumber, melon, squash, etc. Tobacco-dust, bone-flour, ashes, soot, etc., are used to destroy or drive them away, but I have never found anything equal to shell-lime, *air-slaked*, for their destruction.

The Cabbage Flea, a small, black insect, which attacks young plants of cabbage, turnip, etc., is also very destructive, but easily conquered by early applications of the last-named remedy in liberal quantity.

The Cabbage Louse (I use the common names), a small,

bluish insect, often infests crops of growing cabbages. They are not particularly destructive to these, but when a mass of them collect on the heads, as they frequently do, their appearance is spoiled, as they can scarcely be gotten off without removing all the outer leaves, and thus damaging the sale. These pests, though not very destructive to the growing cabbages, are very much so to the plant when producing seed. It was only a few years ago that I had a crop of seed cabbages *entirely* destroyed by them. They first appear, in small clusters, at the tip of the branches about the time the blossoms are coming, and if not immediately attended to, soon envelop the leaves and stalks to their total destruction.

They are generally the worst in dry seasons, and sometimes a heavy shower, before they get much start, will destroy them. I do not know of any positive remedy; lime will check but not destroy them. As soon as they appear on seed-cabbage, the tip on which they lodge must be nipped off, and attention must be paid to them every day until the stalks and pods are quite hard.

A new enemy to the cabbage family has lately appeared in the form of a green grub, which eats away the leaves, and in some sections whole fields have been destroyed. There is no positive remedy yet found against them, though many have been tried, with varying success. They are not yet common in this section, hence I have not had occasion to experiment with them.

Another very injurious insect is the one which produces what is known as "club-root" in cabbages, cauliflower, etc. Various theories have been advanced as the cause of this malformation, but it is, beyond a doubt, caused by a maggot which eats into the root, causing it to swell in various shapes, and destroying the plant. I have no doubt that the eggs are deposited in the manure, and so taken to the field; the maggot there hatches, and at once commences the work of destruction. My conclusions in this matter have been arrived at from observations made on three different crops of radishes, and here, to be the better understood, I will say I believe the Cabbage Maggot and the Radish Maggot to be one and the same.

A few years ago I sowed three pieces of land with the White Summer Radish, one on land manured with stable manure at the time of sowing, the next without manure, where a liberal application had been made the previous year, and the other without manure, but on one end of the land a heap of stable-manure had lain during the winter, and was removed to adjacent land for an early crop. The radishes on the first piece were mostly maggot-eaten; those on the second were not affected in the least, nor yet were those on the third bed, *except where the manure heap had been.* The theory that hog-manure will produce club-root is not entirely unfounded; for, while it may not be the immediate cause, yet no doubt, from its nature, it is the most attractive to the fly in seeking a place to deposit her eggs, and by it more are carried to the ground than in horse or cow manure. I firmly believe that much depends on the previous treatment of manure, such as heating, turning, etc. (by which the eggs may be destroyed), for the prevention of club-root.

Shell-lime is an effectual preventive, and about Newark, N. J., market-gardeners apply it heavily once in about five years with good results.

Undoubtedly the maggots are killed by it before they can begin the work of destruction. Where lime can not be had conveniently, and even where it can, I advise putting the manure, especially that intended for cabbages and cauliflower, into a large heap, letting it heat, and occasionally working it over to prevent scorching.

Henderson advises bone-flour as a remedy for club-root. One thing is certain, if my view is correct; we have in this valuable fertilizer the best substitute for stable-manure, and one that is free from the eggs which produce the Cabbage Maggot.

COLD-FRAMES OR COLD-BEDS.

These are constructed of common plank, usually about twelve Inches high at the back, and eight inches at the front; in width according to the length of the sashes to be used, and in length to suit the number of sashes required; the planks must be supported by durable posts firmly set in the ground, to which they are nailed. They should always be erected in a sheltered position, facing southward, if possible, and on ground nearly or quite level, or perhaps gently sloping to the south. Some use slides upon which to run the sashes up and down; these are very convenient. They are placed at such a distance apart that the edges of the sashes rest on the slides, and are separated by a narrow strip, thus making the operation of airing quite easy. The slides are dovetailed into the plank; hence they are held firm, and yet can be readily removed when occasion may require. The soil of a cold-bed should be light, dry, and free from stones, and enriched according to its intended use; for if designed only as a place in which to preserve plants during winter, moderate fertility is all that is required; but if used for growing and forcing crops for market, it must be made and kept rich by liberal applications of fertilizers.

The soil should be spaded deep and finely pulverized twice before planting, adding well-rotted stable-manure and bone-flour, which should be thoroughly worked into the soil in quantity according to the intended use of the bed, the surface finely raked, and the front *slightly* raised. This is from the fact that the sashes inclining to the front carry the water that way, more or less leakage taking place, beside the lower board shading inside of the frame renders the lower part wet and cold, and a little elevation of soil here has a good effect. Cabbage, cauliflower, and lettuce plants are preserved in cold-beds, which renders them hardy and capable of being transplanted very early in the spring, and to be harvested in time to allow a second crop to be grown on the same ground.

The seeds should be sown about the middle of September, and to make a sure thing it is best to sow on the tenth and again on the twentieth of the month, each time using more seed than sufficient to produce the requisite number of plants. I might here add that cabbage and cauliflower seed will give about three thousand and lettuce-seed six thousand plants to an ounce.

Select a piece of good soil; plow or spade to a depth of eight inches; make the surface fine and even by thorough raking; spread the seed thin over the entire surface, and cover by raking in or sprinkling fine soil over the whole to a depth of one half an inch, slightly pressing with the back of the spade, and if the earth is dry sprinkle with water in the evening. As soon as the plants have formed the second leaves, or become large enough to handle conveniently, they should be transplanted into the cold-frame, the soil being prepared as above directed, and it will be found advisable to prepare the bed just immediately preceding the transplanting, the soil then possessing a natural moisture, which is a condition far preferable to that presented when the surface has become dry, and one which can not be obtained by artificial watering.

It is very important here, as in all transplanting, that the earth be firmly pressed against the root. Cabbage and cauliflower must be set down to the first leaves, or as deep as possible without covering the hearts. By doing this, the stalk is more thoroughly protected, and in case the plants become severely frozen, the frost will draw out through the earth, and they will not be injured as when exposed directly to the sun and air.

Lettuce, however, must not be planted very deep; if the whole of the root be covered, it will be quite sufficient.

The plants may be shaded for a day or two, and if the earth is dry a light sprinkling of water may be given, but this will not be necessary if the earth is fresh and has been pressed firmly to the roots. The plants may be set two and a half by two inches apart; but they will be stronger and better by setting three inches each way, except lettuce, which will have ample room at the distance first named. They should remain exposed until the approach of severe weather, when the sashes must be put on, and during very severe frosts beds of cauliflower may be further protected at night by mats, old carpet, or the like thrown over the sashes. Always bear in mind that these plants are placed in the cold-frame for preservation, and not to make growth; hence, after they have become rooted, the bed must be kept rather dry than otherwise, and the most important point of all is, to give an abundance of air. Whenever the thermometer, *in the shade* on a still day, shows ten degrees, the sashes may be pushed down one or two inches from the top; at twenty degrees, they may be pushed down nearly half-way, and at thirty degrees they can be drawn entirely off. Where slides are not used the sashes may be raised by means of wedges placed under the upper end to correspond as nearly as possible with the above.

These plants are almost hardy in the open ground, and as the glass over them concentrates the sun's rays and heats the air in the bed, great care must be taken lest the plants become drawn thereby. There is much greater danger of keeping them too warm than too cold.

Especially is it very important that they should be exposed for a fortnight before setting in the open ground, and if they have been kept cool and not drawn, the frames may be left open during frosty nights to harden the plants, guarding against snow, which would be liable to destroy some of the plants by breaking the hearts. To guard against the possibility of this, where sashes are removed to use on other frames, it is well to have at hand a supply of shutters, of the same size as the sashes.

Cold-frames are extensively used about New-York City for forcing lettuce, cucumbers, and parsley, and may be used to advantage for producing cabbage, cauliflower, lettuce, and celery plants early in the spring, sweet-potato plants later, herbs for transplanting, forcing beets, carrots, and radishes, forwarding cucumbers, melons, squashes, and lima beans for transplanting to the open ground, and hardening off tomato, pepper, and other plants, all of which are duly noticed under their respective heads.

HOT-BEDS.

These differ from cold-frames mainly in being mostly composed of partly fermented stable-manure, which gives off great heat, and when properly worked and compactly formed continues to do so for a long time, and this, with the assistance of the sun, the heat of which is concentrated by the glass of the sashes, enables us to force or hasten the growth of many vegetables much in advance of the natural seasons, and further aids us in growing such vegetables as are natives of a tropical climate, by forwarding the plants, and which on account of the shortness of our seasons could not be successfully grown, if the sowing of the seeds of such was delayed until the earth had become sufficiently warmed to allow them to germinate.

There are various ways of making a hot-bed, but I will only describe the two leading methods. A stationary hot-bed is made by digging a pit about two and a half feet deep, boarding up the sides and ends to about one foot above ground on the back and three inches on the front, in width and length according to the size and number of the sashes to be used, and furnished with slides, as in the cold-frame, to assist in giving air, etc. Into this pit place one foot of leaves or coarse litter, and manure to a depth of one and a half foot, which must be trodden down rather firmly, the surface made even, and covered with from three to six inches of soil, as the case may require. This style is best suited for forcing lettuce, rhubarb, asparagus, dwarf cabbages, and such vegetables; but I much prefer for general use the movable hot-bed, which is made by excavating one and a half foot deep, two feet wider than the frame to be used, and two feet longer than will accommodate two frames of four sashes each, and not boarding up. In this pit place one foot of leaves or coarse litter, and on that one foot or more of manure, well shaken up, but do not tread it down—the only pressure necessary being a light patting with the back of the fork to even the surface. Throw two planks across on which to walk, and stepping on them, place on the frames, one foot from either end, and leaving one foot on the outside, back and front; square the frame by means of a sash; put in three inches of soil, filling mostly around the sides and ends, to assist these parts in settling, as the center will naturally settle first; put on the sashes, bank up the outside, especially on the north, with coarse manure. Choose a mild day for the work, and let it be done as expeditiously as possible, that the manure may not be too much chilled.

The object of having the pit wider than the frame, is to allow the manure, earth, and frame to settle *evenly* in a body. The frames can be made from ordinary thirteen-foot plank, accommodating four sashes, six by three feet, with sliders, without waste, and will be full heavy enough for two men to handle, being two planks on the back and one on the front, braced with pieces of joist in the corners and center, to which the planks are nailed, the ends being raised the thickness of the sashes.

The sliders can be dovetailed in the same as the cold-frame and the frames made without bottoms. By either method, when the bed has stood three days, the sashes and sliders should be removed, the soil raked even and fine, and as much more added as may be necessary, which will depend on the crop to be grown, directions for which are given under each separate head.

It is very important to have good manure, and to have it well worked over before using, to insure success in making a hot-bed. Manure as it comes from the stables is generally too coarse, and makes too rank a heat. It should be thrown in a heap, and when heated, which may be known by the vapor arising from it, the whole must be turned and forked over, and this sometimes repeated four or five different times, but usually three good workings will temper it, the last being given three or four days before it is to be used. The manure that is shipped from New York City, by boat and railroad, is generally in good condition for making a hot-bed.

The soil should be light, free, and moderately rich, though I have found that which has long been used, to have a tendency to cause the young plants to damp off, and I would recommend using one half well-rotted sods and one half old soil, thoroughly mixed.

Select a sheltered, warm position for a hot-bed, and one that may be permanent, as the same pits or trenches last from year to year, the earth and manure being removed to a heap, and the frames, if movable, snugly stored away to do duty again the following and many successive years.

FORCING-PIT.

This is an arrangement similar to the stationary hot-bed frame, and can be used for forwarding rhubarb, cauliflower, cabbage, etc., without resorting to the use of hot manure, and sometimes a frame is used, the same as a movable hot-bed frame, but built one plank higher back and front. Directions for using are given under the head of such vegetables as are grown in this manner.

TOOLS AND THEIR USES.

The tools required in gardening and seed-growing are quite numerous.

Various patterns of different kinds have been invented, some improvements on the old style, but many of no practical value. I shall avoid as much as possible recommending any particular pattern of either tool of which I make mention, but leave the selection to the judgment of those who may have occasion to use them; because what suits one may not suit another.

Plow.—Use a plow which will positively invert, that is, completely turn over the soil. Take a narrow furrow, and while it is important to plow deep, yet it is not expedient to do so until the land is made comparatively rich. Plow, five or six inches deep, following with the subsoil plow to a depth of six inches more. At the next plowing run the surface plow deeper, and so continue each time until a depth of ten inches or more is attained, frequently applying manure, without which deep plowing is injurious, but with it vastly beneficial.

Subsoiling may be done frequently with good results, and the depth increased gradually to eighteen inches.

Harrow.—The most suitable harrow is made square, about five and a half feet either way, with four cross-pieces, which, with the front and back, each contain alternately eight and seven teeth, nine inches apart, set diagonally, so as to cut four and a half inches.

The teeth should be made of one-inch square iron, pointed and hardened, and the points should project eight inches and the heads one inch.

The ground should be twice gone over, then reverse

the harrow and "back it." This will generally make the surface fine, but if not, go once more over with the teeth and again with the back of the harrow. When the ground is in fit condition to work, it can be made sufficiently fine and even by skillful "back-harrowing," to admit of sowing nearly all kinds of seeds, but occasionally to get a bed in prime order the surface must be well raked.

Cultivator.—The "harrow-tooth" cultivator is requisite in garden crops while the plants are small.

Afterward, the "broad-toothed" or any of the improved styles may be used, always going twice each way.

Always bear in mind that the "cultivator" is better to prevent than to destroy weeds, so commence early and repeat often; never wait until the weeds can be seen.

Hoe.—The operation of hoeing is, in gardening, a very important one.

It is necessary to hoe deep to loosen the soil; and thoroughly pulverize it to effectually destroy young weeds.

A steel-toothed rake may be used in the manner of a hoe to advantage in disturbing the soil before the weeds get any start, which, by the way, should never be allowed. The "pronged hoe" is effectual in loosening the soil and preventing the weeds growing; taken in time, more work can be done with one than with a common hoe in the same time. The "push or scuffle hoe" is very useful for loosening the surface soil, between rows of small plants before the other hoes can be used, and some crops can be worked almost entirely with them. They are also useful in cleaning ground for a second crop. Sizes vary from four to twelve inches, all of which are useful.

Spade.—Spade cultivation is no longer considered the one great point in gardening. Henderson very truthfully remarks, "No digging in the ordinary way can pulverize the soil so thoroughly as can be done by the plow and harrow, nor no trenching much surpass in its results that done by thorough subsoiling." Still, cold-beds and small pieces of ground must sometimes be dug, and it is advisable that it be done well. Never set the spade far back; or, in other words, take a little earth at one time, invert it, and pulverize well with the spade, if one is used, but the "spading-fork" will be found a good substitute, and much better for this purpose.

Rake.—The ordinary wooden rake contains ten teeth; those best adapted to garden use have fourteen. In covering seed, rake lengthwise with the rows, taking from two to four rows together, breaking lumps with the back of the rake. In smoothing the surface for sowing, rake as much as possible from the sides, to avoid unnecessary treading over the bed. Steel rakes have fine sharp teeth, and are very useful where it is important to have the surface soil extra fine. When used as a substitute for the hoe, various sizes are necessary to accommodate the width between the rows.

Garden-Line.—This is very essential where straight rows are desired, and such certainly always should be.

Let the line be strong, though not heavy, as long as the lands, and for convenience be wound on a reel, and have a sharp-pointed iron at each end for fastening into the earth. To get the line *perfectly* straight, set the pin at one end, unreel the line, draw it *tight*, and fasten the reel-pin firmly in the earth; return to the center, raise the line with the thumb and finger, four or five feet from the ground, and let it quickly descend—using the line in fact in the same manner as a carpenter uses a chalk-line.

Markers.—These are indispensable in marking rows for sowing seeds or setting plants. To make them, take a piece of 4x4 joist six and a half feet long, to which attach a handle and cross-piece, the whole forming the letter T.

To the joist, or head, nail strips two inches wide, projecting six inches, and slightly sharpened at the ends. Two markers are requisite, on one of which set the strips or teeth, ten inches apart on one side, and fifteen inches on the reverse. On the other set the teeth on opposite sides, twelve and eighteen inches apart.

By this plan four markers are combined in two, and facilities are afforded for marking rows ten, twelve, fifteen, and eighteen inches apart, or the spaces may be varied to suit.

A more durable marker can be made by having light, flat iron teeth, but in this case the frame must not be so heavy, and the whole may be iron-braced.

In marking rows, first draw the line straight at one side of the bed, and walking backwards, draw the marker along, keeping the outer tooth nearly up to the line; then set the outer tooth in the inner mark, and return, and so continue until the land is finished.

By care, a broad bed can thus be marked out, and the rows all be straight, by once stretching the line. These markers can be used for wide planting, as, for instance, cabbages at thirty inches; use the fifteen inch side and plant the alternate rows.

Dibble.—The best dibble or implement for transplanting can be easily made from a natural bent limb of a tree—apple generally affording the best. It should be ten inches long, with the crook for the handle four inches more; the main part one and a half inch in diameter at the centre, and from there gradually tapering to a point, which should be lightly ironed and the whole made smooth. This style is far preferable to the old one, made from the upper part of a spade-handle.

Seed-Sowers.—These are very useful, doing the work easier, quicker, and in most cases better than by hand.

They are regulated generally by changeable slides, containing holes nicely graded as to size, and directions for setting to sow the different seeds accompany each machine; but as "circumstances alter cases," it is best not to pay too much attention to these instructions.

The best way is, to spread a cloth and sow some seed on it, varying the grade to suit the seed and the quantity required. All sticks and chaff should be removed from seed before sowing it by machine.

Forks.—The most convenient fork for handling manure is one that is light, though it must be strong. When a fork is used to separate stalks from seed after thrashing, one with very few tines should be used, that the seed may be thoroughly shaken out, but it is advisable to do this work by the hands alone.

Shears.—The spring shears, such as are used for pruning, are very useful for cutting seed-stalks, and are far preferable to a knife. Sickles make quicker work than shears in cutting the stalks of cabbage or turnip seed, but there is more jar, which causes some loss of seed, and upon the whole shears may be considered the best implement for cutting seeds.

Trowel.—This is an important implement in lifting plants, when a ball of earth is required, attached to the roots. It is also useful in taking up dry onions, especially "sets," and very handy to assist in transplanting egg-plants, tomatoes, etc., which are taken up with balls of earth.

Straw Mats.—These are very useful for protecting hot-beds and cold-frames, and covering onions, onion sets, etc.

The usual size is five by seven feet. To make them, erect a frame in the market-house, or some out-building, using for the sides common boards set edgewise against the wall or partition, with a piece of joist at the top and one near the floor at the bottom.

The frame should be five feet wide, and in hight from

the floor to the ceiling. In each piece of joist firmly set iron staples one foot apart and six inches from either side. From the lower staples to the upper ones firmly stretch strings of tarred marline, seven feet long. Make a straw band five feet long and one inch thick, by firmly wrapping the straw with tarred string. Fasten the band securely at the bottom of the upright cords by means of tarred strings, which for convenience' sake may be wound on sticks, and must be attached to the uprights, and afterwards serves for binding the straw.

Supposing two men to be engaged at this work, which is the most expeditious plan, let each be provided with a bundle of straw, and taking sufficient to make an inch in diameter when bound, place the but-ends against the frame on each side, and wrap the tarred strings around the straw and the upright at the same time, passing it through in the form of a half-hitch, and draw it tight. To make the strings draw easy, rub them with soap. When the desired length is completed, put on a band as in the start. It is very important to have good rye straw for this purpose.

It should be reaped, and hand-thrashed, or, what is better still, be reaped when in blossom, whereby it does not require thrashing, hence is much stronger, and moreover does not contain any grain to attract mice when the mats are stored.

Straw mats, if rolled up and stored away when out of use, and temporarily put away during wet weather, when in use, will last a great many years.

Sashes.—These are very important. They may be made of any convenient size. Those generally used by gardeners are three by six feet, the frames of clear pine, an inch and a half thick; the glass six by eight inches, and of the best quality. By keeping them glazed and painted they will last many years.

2*

Shutters.—These are made of worked ceiling boards, of the same size as the sashes, and are battened the same as a door. They are very convenient to put over plants in the frames, from which the sashes have been removed, in case of sudden cold or storm, and can also be used over the sashes in cold weather as a protection. They are very convenient to dry seeds on, and may be put to a variety of uses.

Wheelbarrows.—The person who has vegetables to prepare for market, will find these very convenient in bringing the produce from the field to the market-house, also in moving plants of egg-plant, tomato, etc., from the hot-beds to the ground, and there are numerous times when the wheelbarrow is quite as important as the wagon to the gardener. Those generally used by market-gardeners are of the box pattern, and usually twice as large as those sold in the stores.

Fan-Mill.—This to the seed-grower is very valuable, and it is important to have sieves for it of every grade, to accommodate seeds of any size or weight. In cleaning seeds with the fan-mill, let them run slowly and evenly, and regulate the sieves according to the size of the seed, and the force of wind according to its weight; light seeds requiring a light wind, and *vice versa*.

Sieves.—These are also indispensable in cleaning seeds, as many kinds can not be thoroughly cleaned by the fan-mill. It is well to have a full set, from No. 2 to No. 40. The numbers are in accordance with the meshes to a square inch, and from No. 8 upwards should be of brass wire, as those of fine iron wire soon rust out.

Cloths.—Cloths for gathering seeds, etc., are very useful, and it is well to have a good supply. A cloth the full size of the thrashing floor is useful in saving seed, unless the joints are very tight, and even then the seed can be more readily handled, and is not so liable to be broken when on a cloth as when thrashed on the bare floor. Another cloth, sufficiently large to cover the bottom and sides of a wagon, is necessary in carrying seeds from the field to the barn to be thrashed, and may also be used for covering vegetables when being transported by wagon. This and the preceding one should be made of light cotton-duck; sometimes old sails can be had sufficiently sound to answer the purpose. "Hand-cloths" nine feet square are useful for carrying seeds. These should be made of an article called "burlaps," except such as are only used to dry seeds on, which may be of strong muslin.

Wagons.—Market-gardeners who convey their produce directly to market, use spring wagons, made very strong, to carry a heavy load of vegetables, and bring back a load of manure. Such a wagon will be very useful to the farm-gardener, in conveying produce to the point of shipment, and also to the seed-grower in carrying seeds, etc., from the field to the barn, and for sundry other purposes; but in these cases, the latter especially, it need not be so heavy. A convenient size is one large enough to carry ten barrels, with high body and flaring side-boards. For carting manure, farm wagons are certainly the best, when conveying it any considerable distance, but for this purpose, at home, dumping carts are far preferable.

Buildings.—Good comfortable stables and barn room, as well as sheds for wagons, plows, sashes, mats, etc., are indispensable, and in addition, those who grow vegetables for market will need a place wherein to prepare stuff for market, and water convenient is necessary, for such things as require washing. This building, generally called the "market-house," should be of good size, and may be used for storing those of the smaller tools which are frequently needed.

The upper part will be very convenient for storage purposes. A good cellar beneath will not be amiss,

The seed-grower requires a room similar to this in which to work wet days, clean seeds in winter, etc., and in addition, a dry, well-ventilated room for storing, and an abundance of loft room for drying seeds, all of which should be so constructed as to be free from mice and rats, which make sad havoc among seeds when they once get in. Seed lofts should be divided, to prevent the seeds becoming mixed, by any means, while drying.

STORING ROOTS FOR WINTER.

Many roots are the most salable in winter, when there are no green vegetables, and many seed crops require the roots to be carefully preserved from frost during winter and transplanted sound in the spring. To preserve them properly is an important matter. The most natural and the simplest plan, is to put them in pits. These should not be very deep, nor very long, as it is not advisable to store many in one bulk. A good size is one that will hold about thirty-five bushels, twelve feet long, two feet deep, two feet wide at the bottom, and two and a half feet at the top. The pit should be filled rather more than even-full, covered with six inches of straw and eight inches of earth, which must be packed firm to turn the water.

"Chimneys" of straw may protrude from the center for ventilation, but if the bulk is small and the roots are perfectly dry when put away, this will not be necessary. At the approach of severe cold weather, the covering should be increased to eighteen inches, or at least enough to keep out the frost.

Root-cellars were formerly used to some extent, and will yet be found very convenient, where small lots of roots are frequently wanted. They can be made by digging, say six feet deep, any length and breadth, setting posts and boarding up the sides, covering with a strong roof, over which put twelve inches of soil and sod the whole.

The door should be to the southward, and so arranged as to be covered in severe cold weather. No windows are necessary, as all roots keep best away from the light. The inside may be divided into bins, of any convenient size, but here, as in pitting, it will be advisable not to put too many roots in one bulk. An ordinary cellar can be used, if free from frost and yet not over-warm; but the main difficulty generally is, cellars are too dry, and there is too much light. Roots will keep well in a cool cellar, placed in heaps, and covered with thin sods.

Onions should be kept in a dry loft, well ventilated, and spread thin until settled cold weather, when they may be put thicker, and covered with straw mats, straw, or hay. They must not be disturbed while frozen, nor the covering removed until they become thawed out away from the light and air. Directions for preserving green roots, such as celery, etc., are given under their respective heads.

HARVESTING AND CLEANING SEEDS

Particular attention must be paid to these two points. Seeds, to look well, should be perfectly clean, entirely free from chaff, sticks, sand, and all foreign matter, and in cleaning, much depends on how they have been harvested.

Beans, peas, etc., will be more or less damaged in appearance if exposed to rains after they are ripe; so also will wet weather injure seeds of cabbage, turnip, etc., by destroying the color, and causing some to sprout if long exposed.

In fact, all seeds have a much brighter appearance when harvested as soon as ripe, than when allowed to be weather-beaten. Hence, while it is essential that all seeds should be fully matured, it is also important to gather them as soon as they are ripe.

The thrashing of seeds must be carefully done, to avoid breaking with the flail, and grinding under foot, especially those of a soft and oily nature. Thrashing should be done, so far as practicable, when the air is dry. In fermenting seeds of pulpy vegetables for washing, judgment is required, for while, as a rule, no seeds are injured so far as germinating is concerned so long as they lie in the natural juice, yet if allowed to remain longer than necessary to remove the mucilaginous covering they soon lose color.

In washing, it is very essential that it be done in the early part of a clear day, that the seeds shall not be long wet by water, lest some may sprout, and hence be spoiled. Never put seeds away in bulk, until they are *thoroughly* free from moisture.

FALL PLOWING.

I desire to call the attention of those who till the soil, especially those who may go into the business of farm-gardening or seed-growing, to the importance, in my opinion, of plowing land in the fall. The subject has been discussed at various times, and while some have asserted that it is productive of but little or no good results, yet there are some who deem this practice of great importance as being vastly beneficial to the soil.

It is the custom almost universally among market-gardeners, with whom it is important to have the soil fine and free from lumps, to plow their ground deeply and harrow thoroughly after the crops have been removed in the fall, for they understand full well there is nothing which will so completely aid in pulverizing the soil as the action of frost, and being loosened by the plow, the frost can act more effectually during the winter; and moreover, the sun acts more forcibly upon it in the spring; consequently, it thaws quicker, and can be worked earlier than when left as the previous crop was taken from it.

Some contend that on fall-plowed land the snows of winter are as beneficial as an ordinary dressing of manure, and while I can not vouch for the truth of this, yet there can be no doubt that the snow collects and brings with it the gases and impurities floating in the air, which may be beneficial to the soil, and can, of course, become more thoroughly impregnated where the land is newly plowed.

One thing is positively certain, that land plowed in the fall or early winter can be plowed again in the spring earlier and easier and more free from lumps than that not fall-plowed, and this with the comparative ease with which it can be worked during the summer will more than compensate for the time consumed in extra plowing, to say nothing of the increase of crops brought about by the land being in suitable condition for the roots to take hold, and to find nourishment for the growing plant.

VEGETABLES AND THEIR SEEDS.

ASPARAGUS.

The increasing demand and consequent high prices obtained for this vegetable, as well as its availability for transportation, render it an object worthy the attention of the farm-gardener. Quantities of it are being annually planted at the east end of Long Island, where the character of the soil and the humid, saline air seems particularly adapted to its growth. As a general rule, asparagus succeeds best near the sea-coast, though it can be (and is) profitably grown far inland, and upon almost any soil, by proper preparation and careful attention, and in fact this is a very essential point and the great secret of success in any locality. Those who contemplate growing this vegetable for profit will do well to bear in mind the latter fact; and, moreover, it matters not how well the bed may have been prepared and enriched in the beginning, unless it is kept up to a high state of fertility by annual applications of manure in liberal quantity and thorough working, all preliminary labor will have been in vain. An asparagus bed, thoroughly prepared and properly attended to, will continue to yield in large quantity for an indefinite number of years, most writers placing the time at twenty, but I have known of at least one bed producing profitably for thirty years from the time of planting.

Growing the Plants.—The soil best adapted to growing asparagus roots or plants is a deep loam where sand predominates, and which has been well manured the preceding year. Give a good dressing of stable-manure, plowed under, or bone-dust, bone-phosphate, or guano harrowed in. The ground should be deeply and thoroughly plowed, and harrowed fine. Mark out rows fifteen inches apart, about two inches deep, and sow the seed in them evenly and thinly as early in the spring as the ground can be worked. If the plants are to be used when one year old, thin to three inches apart as soon as they are up. If not to be used until the second year, they will not require thinning if evenly sown.

As soon as the plants are up, use a twelve-inch push or scuffle-hoe between the rows, and remove all weeds in the rows by hand, and at the same time thin the plants if it is intended to transplant them at one year old.

About a fortnight after, use the prong-hoe to loosen the soil. Keep free from weeds all the season. Let the stalks remain on the bed until spring to protect the young roots from severe freezing and to prevent the ground from heaving. If the plants are not removed in spring, the only attention required the second season will be to occasionally loosen the soil, and keep them free from weeds.

One pound of seed will produce ten thousand plants. The roots may be obtained from any nurseryman or seedsman if it is desirable to save the time and trouble of growing them. One-year-old plants, or those two years, grown in good soil and not stunted, are the best, though they may be used at three years old.

Soil and Preparation.—Asparagus can be grown in almost any soil, but succeeds best in a sandy loam with deep surface and porous clay or sandy subsoil. It can scarcely be made too rich, nor be too well prepared. It is a rank feeder, and its roots penetrate the earth to a great depth and in every direction; therefore, the more assistance given to the plant by thorough cultivation, the greater will be the product. The land intended for an asparagus-bed should be *deeply* plowed in the fall, using at the same time the lifting subsoil plow, which should go as deep as possible, following with the harrow until the surface soil is finely pulverized.

In the spring, apply well-rotted stable-manure, broadcast, at the rate of sixty-two horse-loads to the acre, or when this can not be obtained use raw bone-dust, two tons to the acre. These two fertilizers may be used together; one half the above-named quantities of each to the acre.

Plow deep, again using the subsoil plow; harrow finely and evenly.

If the ground is poor, use about two barrels of bone-phosphate, or seventy-five pounds of Peruvian guano, to the acre in the rows, applied at the first hoeing.

Planting and Cultivating.—Asparagus may be set in the fall, but it is far preferable to use the fall and winter in preparing the land, carting manure, etc.; thus having everything ready for an early start in the spring, and the earlier it is set out the better. There is a diversity of opinion in regard to the most suitable distance at which the plants should be set to obtain the greatest results.

Some advise setting fifteen to eighteen inches each way, while others argue that better results will be obtained by placing them six feet each way. My own observation and experience convince me that these are opposite extremes. When the bed has been thoroughly prepared by plowing, subsoiling, manuring, and harrowing, mark out furrows five feet apart and about eight inches deep. Set the plants eighteen inches apart, spreading the roots, covering and fastening them firmly, burying the crowns about one inch. At the distance here given, five thousand five hundred and eight will set an acre.

The crown and roots occupying about two inches, the top of the crown (though to be covered only one inch at first) will be about six inches below the level of the surface when the furrows have become filled with earth. As soon as the stalks or young shoots appear, cultivate and hoe, and repeat during the summer, gradually filling the furrows, so that by fall the whole surface may be level.

The object of this plan is to ultimately have the crowns deep, which, on account of the weakness of the shoot the first season, can not be accomplished at the time of planting. In the fall, plow a light furrow to the rows on both sides, previously applying well-rotted manure or bone-dust over the rows. In spring, harrow down level, cultivate and hoe during the summer, never allowing the weeds to get a start. The following or second fall, plow away from the rows on both sides; apply well-rotted manure, compost, or bone-dust in the furrows, and plow back, leaving the earth in ridges over every row, stirring the ground between the rows, and always being careful not to cut or disturb the roots. In spring, harrow down nearly or quite level. This season the strongest shoots may be cut; but avoid cutting many, lest the roots be weakened and thereby permanently injured. Cultivate during the summer as before, manuring the following and every succeeding fall as previously directed. After the third year the asparagus may be cut indiscriminately. Every succeeding spring the earth should be harrowed fine, and may be left slightly raised above the rows, which has a tendency to bring the shoots forward earlier than when grown on a level surface. The stalks should be removed before the seeds ripen and fall, lest they germinate and grow, causing more work, and if the plants are allowed to remain, they will soon make the bed a mass of roots and damage the crop. Coarse salt may be used after the third year at the rate of five bushels to the acre, applied to the rows with the manure, or three times that quantity, broadcast, in the fall. Some argue that a heavier dressing will be beneficial, and even assert that salt may be applied to this crop, broadcast, one half an inch thick over the entire surface.

I would not, however, recommend using more than the quantity first named, and it is very doubtful whether this would be beneficial near the seacoast, where there is a saline atmosphere, except so far as it may have a tendency to destroy weeds.

Cutting and Bunching.—The season of asparagus usually lasts until about the middle of June, but is governed in a great measure by "early peas," for as soon as these become abundant in the markets, there is but little call for asparagus.

There are knives made expressly for cutting asparagus, but I have always found an ordinary long-bladed butcher's-knife to answer every purpose. The person cutting should be provided with a whetstone to keep the knife sharp.

In the early part of the season, asparagus will require cutting only about three times a week, but as the season advances and the weather becomes warm, it will be necessary to cut it every day, and sometimes, when very warm, just after a rain, it must be cut twice in one day.

It should always be cut before the head bursts, as after that time it is useless for marketing. When cutting lay the stalks in handfuls along the rows, afterwards gathering them in baskets, but avoid letting them become wilted after cutting. Wash before tying. Do not suffer asparagus to remain in any other than an upright position for any great length of time, and always pack it upright, for if laid otherwise the heads will turn upwards, thus crooking the stalks or bunches.

In bunching, a frame is used, which is made of two pieces of common board, nailed one against the other at right angles; the one for the back six inches high and twelve inches long, the bottom about ten inches wide and twelve inches long.

In this bottom-piece are placed four light upright stakes about six inches long, about four inches apart each way, in the form of a square, commencing two inches from the back. This is the primitive and cheap style of buncher, now partially superseded by machines constructed of metal, much more convenient than the one described. In either case, across the bottom and between the stakes or metal bands, a string must be laid, and on this lay the asparagus, the heads against the back board, to keep them even until a quantity sufficient for a bunch of the size desired has been placed in. Draw the string tight and tie, cut the bottom or base of the bunch even, remove from the frame, press the string down firm, place a light string above the other near the top, and the bunch is ready for market. The size of the bunch must be regulated by circumstances. The stalks should be cut when about six inches above ground, cutting four inches below, hence averaging ten inches in length, and when trimmed will leave the bunch about nine inches long.

An ordinary bunch is from four to five inches in diameter at the center. Use bass-mat or other flat strings, to avoid cutting the stalks.

Pack the bunches with fresh-cut grass, below and between, in boxes, keeping in an upright position.

Growing for Family Use.—When asparagus is grown for family use only, in small quantities, the rows may be not more than half as far apart as for field culture, in which case the bed must be worked entirely by hand, using the spading fork to loosen the soil.

Seed.—Asparagus produces seed when two years old. When fully developed, the stalks are from five to six feet in hight, with numerous branches, upon which are produced a profusion of bright scarlet berries, containing from three to six seeds each. To save the seed, cut the stalks as soon as the berries are ripe, which may be known by their changing color from green to scarlet, and softening somewhat. The berries may be stripped by hand, or thrashed upon a cloth or floor. After separating from the stalks, place the berries in a barrel or tub, and mash them with a wooden pounder, to break the outer shells, and then separate the pulp from the seed by washing.

When placed in water the seeds will settle, while the pulp and shells will readily pass away in pouring off the water. Repeat the washing three or four times, and the seed will be clean; it should then be placed on boards to dry, in the sun and wind. After the first day remove from the sun, but expose to the air in a dry loft, spread thin, for ten days or more.

The seed retains its vitality from two to three years.

Varieties.—Until quite recently the varieties of asparagus have been mainly designated as "Purple Top Giant" and "Green Top Giant," but there has virtually been but one kind—that growing in heavy soil producing purple, and in loamy soil green, and in very sandy soils very light green or nearly white tops or heads. "Conover's Colossal" is undoubtedly a distinct and improved variety, growing very strong and producing stalks of enormous size. Other varieties are being introduced, and any real improvement will be duly appreciated, but much must depend upon the treatment bestowed upon the plants, of whatever variety.

BEAN.

Bush or Dwarf.—These varieties are available for shipping in the green state, if packed in a manner to prevent heating.

It has generally been conceded that beans, especially the white or pea bean, will grow where the land is too poor to produce anything else; but these, like all other vegetables, will amply repay good treatment.

Soil and Preparation.—Select a piece of warm land, rather light than otherwise; apply twenty two-horse loads of stable manure plowed in, or one thousand pounds of bone-flour, or five hundred pounds of guano, harrowed in.

They may be manured in the row with good compost or well-rotted manure in liberal quantities, but broadcast manuring is preferable. Plow and harrow thoroughly, to make the soil fine and free from lumps.

Planting and Cultivating.—Mark out furrows about four inches deep, two and a half feet apart for the smaller and three feet for the strong-growing varieties, and plant from three to six inches apart in the rows, according to the variety. One to one and a half bushel will plant an acre. The season of planting is after all danger of frost is past, usually about the middle of May in this latitude, and at intervals until August, which is the time for planting what are called "Pickling Beans," used for salting down for winter.

These usually bring as good prices as any, except, perhaps, the very earliest, and some seasons they are scarce and high. For this purpose the Refugee is principally used. In growing for seed, it is best to plant in the first of the season, though they will ripen if sown early in July, but the product will not be so heavy. Work with the cultivator and hoe, and at the final hoeing draw a little earth to the plants, as beans, like peas, produce longer and more abundantly by having the roots well covered.

Preparing for Market.—When marketed green they should be gathered as the beans *begin* to swell in the pods, or a little more than half-grown, never washed, nor yet allowed to become wilted, and shipped in crates or barrels well ventilated, to prevent heating. They are usually sold by the bushel.

Seed.—The manner of growing for seed is the same as for marketing green.

When the pods are nearly dry, the plants must be pulled by the roots, and laid in rows for one or two days, and turned over each day, when they may be thrashed, selecting a dry time, and being careful to avoid breaking with the flail. Heavy rains on them after they are pulled are apt to injure the color and brightness of the seed, hence it is essential to avoid this, if any way possible. After thrashing, spread thin in a loft for two weeks or more, when they may be passed through the fan-mill, and stored in bags or barrels, until required for shipping. They will be much improved in appearance by sifting with No. 5 sieve and removing all imperfect grains by hand.

They retain their vitality two years.

Varieties.—The varieties are numerous, and I will only describe some of the leading sorts.

Early Valentine.—Plant compact and upright, rather dwarf; pods short and round; seeds oblong, sometimes irregular, color pale pink, variegated with bright pink and occasionally white streaks or spots; eighteen hundred of them will measure one quart. One of the most productive of the dwarfs, and perhaps the best early variety for using in the green state.

Early Mohawk.—Plant strong and vigorous, a straggling grower; pods long and flattened; seeds large and flattened, color dull purple, variegated with drab and brown; fifteen hundred of them will measure a quart. Not so early as the Valentine, but more hardy and quite productive.

Early China.—Plant compact and upright, dwarf; pods short and round, seeds short, thick, and round, white with distinct red eye; seventeen hundred of them will measure a quart. A very fine bean to use in the dry state, the only objection being the color of the eye, which spoils the looks when cooked.

Early Newington Wonder.—Plant tall and vigorous, sometimes inclined to run; pods small, seeds small, flattened, drab yellow, brown at the eye. Over three thousand are required to measure one quart.

Refugee, or 1,000 to 1.—Late and very prolific; plant very large and tall, inclined to run; pods long and round; seeds long and thin, nearly round, drab and purple spotted, slightly variegated with dull white; eighteen hundred will measure one quart. One of the very best for using in the green state, extensively grown and sold late for pickling.

White Kidney.—Plant tall and vigorous; pods irregular; seeds white, long, and kidney-shaped; twelve hundred will measure one quart.

White Marrow.—Plant tall and branching, inclined to run; pods rather flattened; seeds white, thick, nearly round; fourteen hundred will measure one quart.

White Soup or Pea Bean.—Plant large, straggling, and inclined to run; pods round; seeds small, white, oblong. Four thousand of them will measure one quart. This and the two preceding varieties are used almost wholly in the dry state, and the latter especially ripens very unevenly, consequently the vines must be pulled when the bulk of the crop is ripe, and laid on boards, or hung on fences, etc., to allow the balance to ripen.

Pole or Running.—The varieties of the Pole-Bean are quite numerous, but the well-known LIMA is the only variety grown to any extent for marketing in this section. The other varieties are fully described in all the leading works on gardening, and as the manner of cultivation is very similar, I will only treat of this one principal variety. The soil should be light, warm, and rich. Plow and harrow thoroughly; mark out furrows five feet apart; place a shovelful of well-rotted manure or compost every three feet in the rows, and thoroughly mix it with earth, raising a broad, flat hill. In the center of this, with the aid of a crow-bar, place a cedar-pole ten feet long, firmly set, and about it plant six or eight beans, placing the eye downward, and the whole barely under ground. These should not be planted until settled warm weather, the twentieth of May being considered full early in this section. When the plants are up nicely, thin to three or four to a hill, and as they advance in growth, train them to the poles, bearing in mind that these, like almost all vines except the hop, take a course *against* the sun, or from right to left, and will not go any other way.

They may be forwarded somewhat by planting under glass in a cold-frame about the first of May, and transplanting when the second leaves have formed. When the form of the beans can be plainly seen in the pods they are ready for market, and may be shipped the same as directed for Bush Beans. If grown for seed or for using in the dry state, they must remain on the vines until the pods become nearly dry; then pick, spread thin in a loft, and when perfectly dry, place in bags; thrash carefully, and avoid heavy blows whereby the seed might be split and spoiled. The seed is easily separated from the chaff by the wind, and readily cleaned with a number three sieve. Should there be any broken or damaged seeds, they must be removed by hand. A quart contains six hundred beans. They retain their vitality two years.

The poles, if properly stored, may be used a great many years.

BEET.

The finer kinds of beets, or such as are used for culinary purposes, can be profitably grown within one hundred miles of our leading markets, or at twice that distance where there is direct communication by water. They will not produce as heavily as the coarser kinds, yet a bushel of beets can be grown quite as cheaply as a bushel of potatoes, and will yield fourfold, averaging one year with another, and they always command a fair price during the fall and winter and early spring months.

Sometimes the prices rule very high, and in case of low prices they can be fed out or sold for that purpose to advantage. It is astonishing how little attention is paid to the cultivation of beets for feeding by the farmers of this country when they can be raised with so little trouble, and the larger varieties yield so enormously. They are very nutritious and healthful for stock, coming in use as they do in the absence of all green or laxative food, which is quite as essential for stock, especially cattle, as for mankind.

Soil and Preparation.—The soil best adapted to beets is a deep, rich, sandy loam. The land should be plowed in the fall if possible, and in the spring have a dressing of at least twenty two-horse loads of stable-manure to the acre, which should be plowed in, or one thousand pounds of bone-flour, or five hundred pounds of guano, harrowed in. The ground should be deeply plowed, finely harrowed and back-harrowed, and if not then free from lumps, be raked by hand.

Sowing and Cultivating.—The land being prepared, stretch the line, and mark with the fifteen-inch marker rows about an inch and a half deep. Sow the seed at the rate of four pounds to the acre for main crop, or six pounds when sown very early, as the spring frosts may destroy a part of the first sown, and cover by raking lengthwise with the rows. For early, sow almost as soon as the ground can be worked, and from then until the first of June. I have known them to do well sown as late as July, but consider the first part of May the best time to put in the main crop.

When the plants are fairly up, use the push-hoe close

to the rows, after which thin by hand to four inches for early, or six inches for late crop.

Those pulled out from the very early crops are sold by gardeners in market as "beet-greens," and usually bring more than enough to pay the labor of thinning. After thinning, work deeply with a pronged hoe, and but little more labor will be required, and this only on late crops, which may need a further push-hoeing, and possibly some hand-weeding again, but a narrow push-hoe must be used, and care taken to avoid cutting the growing root, which would cause it to burst or crack open, and thus be spoiled. To grow for feeding stock, the same preparation of soil is essential. Mark out rows thirty inches apart; sow evenly, and thin to ten inches in the row; this is, of course, presuming that the large varieties will be grown, they being the most profitable for such purposes. Here the ground may be worked with a cultivator, and the thinning done in a great measure by the hoe. It will be advantageous to run the push-hoe along each side of the row before the plants are large enough to admit the use of the cultivator, and thus destroy the weeds in the germ. Some recommend the plan of furrowing out rows three feet apart, filling with rotted manure, and sowing on a ridge formed by covering the manure deeply with earth, raking the top before sowing. This plan answers where the land has been but shallow worked, but where the condition of the soil will admit of deep plowing, or moderately so, the system of broadcast manuring and sowing on a level surface will be found the best.

Preparing for Market.—Early-sown beets are usually pulled when about two inches in diameter. All superfluous leaves and fibrous roots are cut away; the bulbs or roots are carefully washed singly with a soft brush, and tied in flat bunches of five to seven. The main crop is usually harvested about the middle of October, sometimes later, but they must not be allowed to become frosted, as in that case they would be very liable to rot. Twist the tops off by hand, and no further preparation is necessary to fit them for market, as beets sold in bulk are never washed. They may be marketed in bulk at any time during the summer when the leaves begin to dry away, and from thence until the following May. Stored beets, especially towards spring, will start to grow, hence, when they are then marketed, the sprouts must be removed, and at the same stroke of the hand remove all fibrous roots, which will add much to their appearance.

Gathering and Storing.—This process is the same whether intended for market or for seed, except, in the latter case, instead of wringing off the tops they must be cut with a knife, being careful to avoid destroying the heart or center germ, as it is this which produces the main stalk and best seed. Particular care should also be exercised lest they become in the least frosted, for they must be kept quite late in spring, before setting them out. Whether intended for market or for seed, select a dry day, pull the beets, laying them in rows, and cut or wring off the tops, as the case may require.

Handle carefully, and put them away as directed in the chapter on "Storing for Winter," except such as may be required for fall sales, which may be placed in heaps on the surface of the ground, and temporarily covered with leaves and earth.

Seed.—Great pains should be taken in selecting to reserve only such as possess the peculiar marks which distinguish the variety. The foliage of beets will assist in a great measure to make selections, hence it is well to go over the bed, and remove all that show any signs of impurity, before the main crop is pulled. To assist in making this selection, I have described the foliage of the leading varieties. Having pulled and topped the roots as above directed, make the selection for seed before they are removed from the ground, as this is the best and most convenient time. Handle carefully and avoid bruising.

The pitting, covering, etc., are the same as for marketing. The roots for seed-raising should be set out as soon as all danger of heavy frost is past, usually about the first of May. Beets, to produce prime seed abundantly, require rich land, and that which has been manured for a number of years is preferable to highly manuring the season of planting. When the ground is not already rich, apply manure or fertilizers as directed in preparing for the crop of roots. Plow and harrow thoroughly; mark out furrows three feet apart, and set the roots one and a half to two feet apart in the rows, covering the whole to the crown. The round varieties can be set by making a hole with a dibble at the bottom of the furrow, into which the tap-root (or tail, as it is erroneously termed) must be placed, and the earth pressed to it by means of the dibble. The long varieties require the use of a crowbar for opening a hole, the dibble being used to fasten the earth about the root. Care must be exercised in handling not to break off or destroy the young sprouts, which will have formed while the roots have been stored. It is a good plan to plant every fifth row with potatoes, over which to walk when gathering the seed, which requires cutting two or three times, and by this method two rows can be reached from either side, and cut with greater ease, with less loss from stripping out, than when grown in a solid body. Keep free from weeds until the plants have attained a hight of about two feet, when the ridging plow may be used and the earth drawn to the roots with a hoe. After this, in consequence of the plants shading the ground, there will be but little chance for the weeds to grow, and the earth being over the roots, and against the stalks, is a great protection against breaking down by wind or storm.

Where but a few roots are set out to obtain seed for

private use, they may be placed three feet apart each way, and the growing stalks supported by stakes. What is generally known as the seed, is a combination of from three to five irregular grains of a fibrous or woody character, each containing one seed proper; hence, what is termed one seed is in reality capable of producing from three to five plants.

The seed-bearing plant, when fully developed, is about four feet in hight, and throws out numerous branches from the base to the top of the main stalk, and along these branches, the entire length, the seeds are produced, and are quite firmly attached; the larger seeds grow at the base, and they gradually become smaller to the tips. Pinching the tips of these shoots when the seed is forming has a tendency to increase its size toward the point and make the whole more uniform. When about two thirds of the seed on the stalk have become brown and partially dry, all such stalks should be cut, and it is sometimes necessary to cut three different times. When the stalks have been cut two or three days, the seeds will thrash off quite readily, but if allowed to remain until the stalks become dry, these will break up and mix with the seed, causing much inconvenience in cleaning; hence, it is important, while giving the seed a chance to develop, not to allow the stalks to become over-ripe, nor to be too long exposed after cutting. The seed is always ripe before the stalks are dry. Small lots may be stripped by hand, but a quantity can best be removed by thrashing with a flail. When the seeds are separated from the stalks, they should be spread thinly, in a loft, for a week or more, after which they may be run through the fan-mill, and stored in barrels, until wanted for packing, when they should again pass through the fan-mill and be finished with No. 10 sieve, to remove the sand or dust, picking out what sticks there may be, by hand. Beet seed retains its vitality seven years.

VARIETIES.

Early Dark Blood Egyptian.—A new variety, of great value for bunching; extra early, very dark blood, flat at the top and bottom, much resembling in shape the white flat turnip; small tap-root, and short, very dark leaves.

Bassano.—Extra early; outside delicate pink; flesh pale red, sometimes nearly white, and pink mottled and veined; leaves pale red, and red and green mixed, sometimes entirely pale green, but this shows white flesh, and should be discarded in making selections for seed.

Early Turnip-rooted.—A cross between the Bassano and the Turnip Blood, favoring the latter, though rather earlier, but not so early as the former, which, however, it entirely supersedes when it comes to market, which is perhaps one week later; usually rather dark red, sometimes with a perceptible paleness, more noticeable internally than externally, rather flattened at the top, and somewhat so at the root; prime for early bunching and good for winter use; leaves dark red, occasionally streaked or mottled with green.

Turnip-rooted Blood.—A little later than the preceding, of nearly the same shape, more tapering at the root; very dark blood-red; leaves very dark red; the very best round beet for winter use or main crop.

Long Smooth Blood.—Long and smooth, tapering root; leaves, skin, and flesh all very dark red; grows about one half above ground; the very best winter beet for market.

Half Long or Pine-Apple.—Evidently a cross between the Long Smooth and Turnip Blood; rather rounded at the top and tapering to the root; leaves, skin, and flesh very dark blood-red.

The foregoing are the leading market varieties, and below are mentioned the best of the large kinds, such as are usually grown for feeding stock.

White Sugar.—Skin and flesh white; leaves pale green; long irregular thick root, growing much out of ground.

Yellow Sugar.—Same as the preceding, except as to color.

Red Mangel-wurzel.—Skin, flesh, and leaves pale red; long, moderately even in form, quite thick at the root, and grows much above ground.

Yellow Mangel-wurzel.—Same as the above except as to color, and generally more irregularly formed.

BROCCOLI.

So closely allied to cauliflower that I prefer to pass it by, and merely make mention here of the leading varieties—namely: White Cape, Purple Cape, and Early Walcheren. Culture the same as cauliflower.

CABBAGES.

This with market-gardeners is an important crop, and with those about New York, the principal one, as by their method of culture they bring the crop very early into market, thus commanding good prices, and land is cleared off in time to admit of a second crop the same season. The better to be understood by my readers, and to do greater justice to the subject, I will divide it into two parts.

EARLY CABBAGES.

Soil and Preparation.—The soil best adapted for early cabbages is a good, strong, retentive loam, and that with a fair proportion of sand can be used to good advantage, provided the subsoil is not too gravelly or porous; still it is not advisable to use very light soil, nor yet that which is very heavy or clayey, and which has a tendency to pack or bake. The land should be plowed and harrowed in the fall, and if not in a very high state of fertility, a liberal dressing of manure or coarse bone may be turned under at that time to good advantage.

Plow again in the spring, turning under thirty two-horse loads of stable manure to the acre for wide planting, when more is to be applied directly to the plant, to fifty or sixty loads for close cropping. In the absence of stable-manure, apply to the acre one ton of coarse bone in the fall, and one tone of bone-flour or one half a ton of guano, in the spring, harrowed in, or where only enough manure can be had for applying direct to the plants in wide planting, use one half the quantity of bone and guano, *broadcast*, as above directed. I much prefer the plan of heavy manuring and close planting for this crop. For this purpose mark rows thirty inches apart (use the fifteen-inch marker and plant on every other mark), and set the plants sixteen inches in the rows, which will require about thirteen thousand plants to the acre. When grown wide, the land should be lightly furrowed out three feet each way, a half shovelful of well-rotted manure or compost placed where the furrows cross, and thoroughly mixed with the soil by means of a hoe, and the surface gently pressed. Five thousand plants will set an acre planted in this way. By either method, prepare the ground immediately preceding the planting, by a thorough plowing and harrowing, and smooth the surface with the back of the harrow.

Sowing Seed and Growing the Plants. — Cabbage seed germinates quite readily, and there is but little art in sowing it; still, painstaking in preparing the soil, covering, etc., thus giving each seed a chance, will insure a greater number of plants from a given quantity of seed, than if carelessly sown. To get the crop off early, and to grow early cabbages in perfection, the seed should be sown in the fall, and the plants wintered over, as directed in the chapter on cold-frames. This sowing requires some judgment, as it is quite important to have the plants of good size, the better to withstand the winter, and yet they must not be over-large, lest, when planted out in the spring, many of them will run to seed, instead of producing heads.

About New York the plants are mostly pricked out in the cold-frames by or before the twentieth of November. When cold-frames are not used, plants may be had quite early, by sowing the seed in a hot-bed made as described in the chapter on hot-beds, and using about three inches of earth over the manure.

But very little heat is required to germinate cabbage seed, and if the bed is very hot, the plants will grow up slim and spindly, hence great pains must be taken to temper the bed before sowing, and give an abundance of air while the plants are growing, whenever the weather will admit of it. The work of airing can not be regulated by any fixed rule, as hot-beds are made at a season of repeated and often sudden changes, and hence they require almost constant attention. A thermometer set in the center of a bed should range from fifty to sixty degrees for cabbage-plants. Here we generally sow in hot-beds about the first of March, which gives us plants about the tenth of April; and I would here remark, that it is much better to sow the seed say six weeks or more in advance of the anticipated time of transplanting, and grow them slowly and strong, than to defer sowing until late, and then have to force them along, thus making them weak and tender, and unable to endure the sudden changes of the spring weather. It is well to remove the sashes entirely from the bed a few days before transplanting, leaving the plants exposed night and day (except in case of very severe cold or heavy storm, when they may be temporarily replaced), and thus harden them off, that the change may not be too great. The surface should be raked level, and the seed sprinkled even and thin, broadcast—two ounces being sufficient for a four-sash frame, and will produce about six thousand plants—covering lightly with sifted soil, gently pressing with a shovel, and sprinkling with lukewarm water at evening. A good wetting when they are to be pulled for transplanting will soften the ground, and cause the earth to adhere to the roots, and be a general benefit to the plants.

Planting and Cultivating.—I have already stated the plants should be set sixteen inches apart in the rows, but a variation of an inch or two either way, will not make any material difference. When desirable to have them exact, use a marked pole, as directed in the chapter on transplanting. Whether wintered in a cold-frame or grown in hot-beds, the plants should be set out as early in the spring as circumstances will admit of, and those from the cold-frame may be transplanted just as soon as the ground can be worked, as they will not be injured by possible subsequent severe weather, provided they are set deep and the roots firmly fastened. These are two very important points, more fully explained in the chapter on transplanting, and alike applicable to either cold-frame or hot-bed plants. The plants will soon take root, when the harrow-cultivator may be run between the rows, and the ground about the plants *deeply* loosened and made fine, being careful, of course, not to disturb the roots. Just before they begin to form heads, the large-toothed cultivator should pass between the rows, and the hoe again used as before, which is ordinarily all the attention they will require.

Cutting and Marketing.—As a general rule, as is well known, a " cabbage head " should be solid to be marketable, or in fact to be eatable, but about New York those who are fortunate enough to have it well advanced very early, not unfrequently cut a few loads of such as are only an apology for " heads," which bring large prices. When the main crop comes in, it is important that the heads should be fully grown and solid. Cabbages should always, if possible, be cut very early in the morning, before the sun can wilt the leaves, as they then come to market looking fresh and plump. Unlike late cabbages, the early kinds should be cut with several leaves about the head, which gives them a much larger and better appearance. When near a market the heads are loaded in bulk, snugly and compactly, into wagons, and either sold from the wagon to retailers or left with a commission dealer for the same purpose. They can be shipped in crates or barrels, well ventilated, but must not be long packed, as they are very liable to heat.

Seed.—Growing the seed of early cabbages is attended with serious difficulties, the chief of which is to produce the heads at a season entirely adverse to their nature.

I sow three separate times, and as near as may be the first, tenth, and twentieth of June, in the same manner as directed for growing late cabbage plants, except owing to the season I choose a moist piece of ground, and in the absence of rain resort to watering every evening until the plants are up, and occasionally thereafter. When the plants are large enough to handle, they may be set out, but at this season of the year transplanting is not always practicable, hence my reason for making three different sowings, in hopes that we may be favored with rain at such time as one lot or the other will be in condition to set out. A piece of land on which has been grown peas, spinach, or other early-maturing crop is used, being plowed, harrowed, and marked out all ready for such time as the rain may come. The land is well manured, broadcast, for the first crop in anticipation of the second, hence no further manuring is necessary, and in fact I have found that early cabbages grown late, in over-rich ground, are apt to be tender, and do not preserve so well over winter as when less stimulated. Whenever the weather will permit, the plants are set out, in the same manner as directed for spring planting, and worked the same way.

I always wish to get at least a part of the early-sown plants set out, as they get fully headed, and give a chance for a very choice selection for stock seed, while the second or last sown, in consequence of not being quite so hard-headed, generally winter the best, but it requires a more experienced eye to select from those half-headed than from such as are fully developed.

The selections must be made according to the color, size, shape, and general characteristics of the variety. About the first of November another plot of ground is taken—one which has just been cleared of a crop and was well manured in the spring, as I find that cabbage seed does better on such than on freshly-manured land. This is deeply plowed, harrowed, and quite deep furrows marked out, four feet apart. The choice cabbages from the bed are placed in these furrows, eighteen inches apart, and laid parallel with the furrows, at an angle of forty-five degrees, always, if possible, with the head to the north, that the stalk, which is the most tender part, may be the better protected. The earth is drawn in abundantly, and pressed over the root and stalk, and partially over the leaves, which are gathered about and over the head.

Nothing more is required until the approach of severe weather, when with plow and hoe the earth must be drawn over the whole, abundantly over the stalk, and firmly pressed, and sufficiently over the head to protect it from alternate freezing and thawing rather than from the frost. As early in the spring as the ground can be worked, the soil must be removed from the heads by plowing away, and carefully using the hoe; and the outer leaves of the head proper be separated, to allow the heart or center germ or shoot to come through, being very careful not to injure the germ, as this is the all-important part in producing seed. Cultivate and hoe, and when the plants are eighteen to twenty-four inches high, throw the earth to them for support; or what is better still, tie to stakes, but avoid *bunching* the branches; a very convenient plan is to place stakes twelve feet apart along every row, and from one to the other firmly stretch tarred marline or spun yarn, to which the stalks may be attached by bass-mat or other flat strings. This marline may be preserved and used many seasons.

Another plan which I have tried successfully is to mark out deep furrows, four feet apart, running north and south, in which a light dressing of very rotten manure is placed, and with a hoe thoroughly mixed with the soil at the bottom of the furrow, and the plants from the second or third sowing, set therein, eighteen inches apart; in the fall all impure heads taken out, the remainder, without being pulled, bent over and treated in all further respects the same as by the plan above described.

Another plan, and the one best adapted for preserving solid heads, is to put them away as hereinafter described for "late cabbage," or to heel them in thick in a cold-frame, cover with shutters, and set them out and cultivate the same as "late cabbage" for seed, under which head I also give directions for harvesting and cleaning the seed, which operation is the same with early and late.

Varieties.—The varieties of early cabbage are numerous, but there are very few in general cultivation, and I will only notice such as are in favor with market-gardeners.

Early Jersey Wakefield.—On account of the attention this variety is now attracting, a brief history of it may not be amiss here. It was first grown in this country by my uncle, Francis Brill, then of Jersey City, N. J., and by him received from England under the name it still bears, about thirty years ago, and proved to be the best early cabbage of that time, as it is still there, and wherever tried in the vicinity of New York City, and is becoming more popular every year. It was adopted by my uncle, my father, and the few other gardeners about Jersey City at that time, as the standard sort, and from it they grew seed from year to year.

In the course of time, wishing to renew the stock, they sent to Europe direct, as well as through the seedsmen of New York, for a fresh supply of seed of the Wakefield, but what they received then and repeatedly since, under that name, was not the genuine article. In consequence of its having been so long grown from the one stock, it is now more irregular in form than originally, rather improved in size, full as early as ever, and now as then the favorite with all Jersey gardeners, as well as those of Long Island and elsewhere about New York, and it is gaining friends wherever it is introduced.

Head large, conical, sometimes rather rounded or flattened; leaves sea-green; stalk short. In selecting for seed, take only such as have pointed heads of good size, compact leaves, and short stalks.

Early York.—Head of medium size, roundish ovoid, close, and well formed, of a deep green color; but few loose leaves, comparatively smooth on the surface; short stalks.

Large Early York.—Very much the same as the "Early York," except being larger; same shape; thicker head.

Early Ox-Heart.—Head large, conical; leaves compact, light green; stalk short.

Early Flat Dutch.—A cross between the Ox-Heart and Large Flat Dutch. Heads large, round, very solid; leaves sea-green, rather spreading; stalk remarkably short. A fine second early variety. Plants usually grown in hot-beds. If kept in cold-frames over winter are very liable to run to seed, unless they are small and bedded late.

Early Winningstadt.—Second early. Heads large, compact, very pointed; smooth, bright, glossy green leaves; stalk rather short.

LATE CABBAGES.

They are not generally grown by market-gardeners in the immediate vicinity of New York, as it would not pay them near so well as the early, and, moreover, a second crop could not be taken from the ground the same year. They are, however, grown extensively on Long Island, partly within carting distance of New York, and a considerable quantity is sent in from different places by railroad and vessels.

The soil and climate of Long Island seem to suit them, and some of the finest cabbages I ever saw were grown in this section.

In any farming district where late cabbages will succeed well, they are worthy the attention of farmers; for it not unfrequently happens that in the city markets during the fall and winter months they bring very high prices, and almost always sell high enough to insure profit to the grower; but in case of a glut, and consequent low prices, they can be used for feeding stock, and are very valuable for that purpose.

Soil and Preparation.—The remarks on *soil* in reference to early cabbage are equally applicable to the late varieties. The *preparation* must, however, necessarily be quite different, as the late kinds would not pay for such liberal quantities of manure as are bestowed upon the early crop, nor yet do they require it. Late cabbages are grown as a second crop, following early potatoes, peas, spinach, etc., where such things are grown for market, and succeed admirably on inverted clover-sward. On clover-sward or other good land, a dressing of twenty two-horse loads of good stable-manure to the acre, plowed in, one thousand pounds of bone-flour, or six hundred pounds of guano, harrowed in, will bring a good crop; but in the case of stable-manure, if more is at hand, it can be used to advantage, and will be a great benefit to the succeeding crop. Land heavily manured for the first crop will require but little more to bring this one.

A dressing of ashes will also be beneficial, and will have a tendency to destroy the grubs. After plowing, the ground should be well harrowed, smoothed with the back of the harrow, and rows marked out three feet apart. For wide planting, the ground may be furrowed out, and manured in the angles as advised for early cabbages. This planting has to be done in midsummer—usually the first part of July—and it is quite necessary to have the ground all marked out and ready for rainy weather, which at this season is apt to be of short duration, and must be taken advantage of.

Sowing Seed and Growing the Plants.—The seed should be sown the first part of May. It is advisable to sow on the fifth and fifteenth for the main crop, using plenty of seed each time to be sure of a full supply of plants, allowing one ounce of seed for three thousand plants, and if there is any surplus, there is generally a demand for them, or at least enough can be sold to pay the expense of raising. The first sown, if planted early in July, will be headed in the fall, and the later ones answer for winter use, as they keep much better than very hard heads. The seed may be sown broadcast, but I prefer to mark rows ten inches apart, and an inch and a half deep, on a piece of moderately rich light soil, well prepared, in which the seed is deposited rather thinly, and covered by raking in. As soon as the young plants begin to break the soil, sprinkle the bed with air-slaked shell lime, which is to be repeated again when they are nicely up, to prevent the ravages of an insect generally known as the cabbage flea. This must not be neglected, or the entire crop may be speedily destroyed, as they are very destructive, and at times very numerous at this season of the year. (See chapter on Insects.)

Planting and Cultivating.—The directions given under this head in the article on Early Cabbages apply also to these, except the distance.

The rows being already marked three feet apart, the plants should be set two feet in the rows, requiring seven thousand two hundred and sixty to an acre; or at the angles where the manure has been placed and prepared, requiring nearly five thousand plants for the same amount of land. The planting, as I have before stated, should be done in wet weather; but it frequently happens that the rains at this season are not sufficient to thoroughly wet the earth, hence we have to resort to "puddling," which is described in the chapter on transplanting. They should be set out in July, though if in very rich soil, a good proportion will head if set so late as the first of August.

It often happens there is a scarcity of cabbages in market between the seasons for late and early, and those who are far-seeing enough to have an intermediate crop, do well by it. The Large Flat Dutch is a good variety for this purpose, and may be sown at any time after the ground opens in the spring, and if a person should sow three different times, for instance, the first, tenth, and twentieth of April, and from each sowing plant a bed, there would be a chance to make a good hit on at least one lot, and do well on all, and the plants would be ready at a time when a piece of growing clover could be turned under, and a good crop grown with little or no manure. This variety is also used for sowing in hotbeds, and occasionally for keeping over winter in coldframes, and by planting early succeeds the early varieties when the market is not glutted, and sometimes sells at very high prices.

The cultivation of this variety is the same in these cases as when grown for winter.

Cutting and Marketing.—The large or late kinds of cabbage should always be solid, and their fitness for market may readily be determined by pressing the hand on each head.

They should be cut without any superfluous leaves when sent to a city market, but in villages where people have room for the purpose, most persons prefer to buy them in quantity with the roots and leaves attached, that they may be buried and taken out as occasion may require. I might here add that it is customary for gardeners to allow dealers four heads extra to every one hundred, and they in turn allow thirteen to the dozen.

This rule applies generally to all vegetables growing above ground, but not as a rule to roots which grow below.

Storing for Winter.—Cabbages for using or marketing in winter may be put away the same as when intended for seed, described hereafter, but a much easier and quite as good a plan, where the head only is to be preserved, is to make a double row, setting the heads close together on the ground, roots upward, throwing one or two furrows to them on each side, lightly covering and ridging with a spade.

Seed.—Late varieties of cabbage, for seed, are grown in their regular season, in the same manner as for market, and as a general rule the crop is more certain than with the early kinds; hence, the stock of seed is generally abundant, and prices are not so high. It is a good idea to have late cabbages planted early, to make a *choice* selection for *stock* seed; but for the main crop, that which is planted about the twentieth of July, in moderately rich soil, will keep the best, and be sufficiently advanced to make a pure selection. The selections must be made according to the characteristics of the variety, the same as with the early kinds. It may happen that in cutting cabbages, either early or late, there may be some *extra choice* heads from which one would desire to grow seed, but from the earliness of the season and the ripeness of the heads it could not be done in the usual form, as they would not keep until spring. To accomplish this, when the said heads are cut, make a mark with the knife across the top of the stump, and afterwards dig all such stumps and heel them in until fall, when they may be bedded the same as heads. This is known as "stump seed," and while no perceptible difference may be seen in the crop grown from it *one year only*, yet experience has proven that in time it will deteriorate, and the only way to produce prime cabbage-seed is to grow it directly from the head. I never put the heads away where the seed is to grow, as with early cabbage, but prefer to lay them away in a bed.

The latter part of November choose a dry piece of ground running north and south; run a double furrow, throwing up a ridge a foot and a half high. On the east side of the ridge, commencing on the south end, lay the cabbages in a single row, well up to the top of the ridge, and packed close together. While one man is laying them in, another must come behind spading the earth over the roots and stalks, firmly treading it down, while still another follows, throwing more dirt over the roots, pressing it firmly with the foot, filling well under the heads with fine soil, covering the root and stalk about six inches, and leaving the earth in the form of a ridge, as in the beginning. This operation is continued until seven rows are in, each row a trifle lower than the preceding one, so that when the whole is complete there may be descent enough to carry off the water. The earth is firmly pressed against the back of the first row, fine soil put in from each side between the rows, sufficient to make the surface even, leaving the tops of the heads exposed.

The main point is to protect the stalk at junction with the head, as it is here the most sensitive to cold, and must be well covered.

The bed is then banked up, back, front, and ends, to a depth of two feet, or more, and so left until cold weather, when it must be covered with coarse hay, straw, stalks, or brush, lightly, not as a protection against freezing, but to prevent alternate freezing and thawing. As soon as the ground can be worked in the spring the cabbages must be set out, the heads opened, and in all other ways managed as directed for early cabbages, except that they will not require space and earth for ridging, as those planted in the fall. The rows may be only three feet apart, but it is well to give plenty of room, to avoid the intertwining of the branches, and prevent loss of seed, by stripping out in harvesting.

In any event avoid exposing the stalks to the sun, by covering them, as well as the roots, with earth. When the seed is ripe, which may be known by the pods turning yellow, and eventually becoming dry, the stalks must be cut off and laid on the ground for a day or two to dry. It is best to gather it when the pods are yellow, for if allowed to remain until they are dry, the seeds lose color and shrivel up. It will be necessary to make three cuttings to secure a crop in prime order. After the stalks have lain long enough to cause the seed to shell readily from the pods, they can be removed on cloths, or if a large quantity is to be handled use a high-box wagon, covering the sides and bottom with cloths to prevent loss. Carry it to the thrashing floor. But little labor will be required to thrash it out; in fact, the most will shell in the wagon while loading, and care must here be exercised or much may be lost.

When thrashed, remove the stalks, run through the fan-mill, and lay the seed away on cloths, in a loft, for a fortnight, to dry, after which it may again be passed through the fan-mill, and finally cleaned with a No. 18 sieve.

Cabbage seed retains its vitality four years.

Varieties.—As with the early, so with the late cabbage, the varieties are numerous, and I will only describe such as are generally cultivated.

Large Flat Dutch.—Heads large, very broad, and flat, not very thick in proportion; color light green or nearly white at maturity; outer leaves whitish green, not numerous, but somewhat spreading in rich ground; stalk short. A sub-variety of this, known as the "Premium Flat Dutch," has heads more oval at the top, and leaves of dark green. The former is preferred by gardeners.

American Drumhead.—Heads very large, rounding at the top, very thick, tinged above with purple; leaves dark green, profuse and spreading; stalk rather long. Considered the best variety to grow for feeding stock.

Bergen Drumhead.—Heads large, compact, and rounding at the top; leaves rather small, compact, and, as well as the head, distinctly marked with purple; stalk short. A valuable variety for keeping over winter.

Green Curled Savoy.—Head small, yellowish green, very compact and solid, nearly round, a little pointed at the top; leaves small, few, and compact, dark green; stalk short. May be planted closer than the Drumheads or Flat Dutch.

Drumhead Savoy.—Similar to the above in most respects; head large, and flattened at the top; leaves rather more spreading. The Savoys are the best keepers and decidedly the finest flavored of all cabbages, not as extensively grown as their good qualities warrant, but gaining popularity every year.

Red Dutch.—Head medium size, round, extremely solid; leaves few, and, like the head, in color very dark red or purple; stalk moderately short. Used for pickling, and for this purpose usually in fair demand, and prime heads always command good prices.

Turnip-rooted or Kohl-Rabi.—This is intermediate between the cabbage and turnip, and though classed with the former has more the appearance of the latter. The stalk just above the ground swells out, forming a round fleshy bulb, from which the leaves start separately, and the whole has much the appearance of a Ruta-Baga turnip. It can be sown in cold-frames as soon as the cabbage plants are removed, and transplanted to the open ground when large enough to handle, about eighteen inches apart each way. For late crop they are sown in June, and transplanted as above, or may be sown in rows and thinned out, which is preferable to transplanting in hot weather. In either case they require rich soil, and to be well worked. In marketing, the root and superfluous leaves are cut away, and three or four bulbs tied in a flat bunch.

The seed is obtained by preserving the bulbs and roots over winter in a cellar or pit, and transplanting in the spring, cultivating the same as directed for Ruta-Baga.

CAULIFLOWER.

Where this vegetable does well, there is certainly no crop which will pay a larger profit. For the past two years the farmers of the east end of Long Island, especially about the village of Mattituck, have planted largely of cauliflower, being incited by the successful experiments of some who have removed here from the west end, who were formerly engaged in growing vegetables for New York markets. The past season the crop has succeeded admirably, and large profits have been realized by growers in this vicinity, and this by men many of whom are inexperienced in the cultivation of this or any other vegetable for market, and moreover the most of it was grown at the worst possible season of the year. As a general rule cauliflowers do not succeed well on old land, and much of the land hereabouts is new, and but very little of it indeed has ever been used for cabbages or anything of this nature. But, beyond a doubt, it is the humid, saline atmosphere of this section, which makes the cultivation of this vegetable a success. Protracted drouths are here almost unknown, and even during the temporary absence of rain in the summer months, the air does not seem so dry and withering, so to speak, as in sections more remote from the ocean, the Sound, and the great salt-water bays by which we are surrounded.

Soil and Preparation.—Cauliflowers require a deep, strong, and rich soil to be grown in perfection, and that which has been recently broken up, or at least upon which no cabbages, turnips, nor anything of this nature has been grown, or has been for some time seeded down, is preferable to land long tilled. The soil should be prepared and the crop cultivated as directed for early cabbages. The early dwarf varieties may be set thirty by eighteen inches, but the leading growers here seem to think they will not blight so readily when planted wide, and recommend setting the early sorts three feet and the late ones four feet apart each way. They, however, do not sow until spring, and if the plants are kept over in cold-frames, and transplanted early, as they should be, the dwarf kinds can be set out at the first-named distance. The great drawback to the successful cultivation of this vegetable in most parts of our country, is undoubtedly the heat and drouth of our summers, hence it is best to plant very early to get ahead of the heat, or otherwise at such time as will bring the *heading* after the intense heat is past. To accomplish the first, sow in the fall and keep the plants over winter as directed in the chapter on cold-frames, and treat afterwards the same as directed for early cabbage. The seed of the late varieties may not be sown until near the first of June, then in the manner directed for sowing seed of late cabbages, and the after-cultivation is similar to that for this crop. Extra manuring will, however, be very beneficial. When the cold-frame is not at command sow in early hot-bed, the same as directed for early cabbages, and endeavor to have the plants grown and hardened by the time the ground is fit to work, and get them out as early as practicable.

Plants may also be grown by sowing in the open air, as soon as the ground can be worked; but in the latter case, the heads will be forming at midsummer, and there are few sections where they will do well at this season of the year.

Late cauliflowers which have not perfected their heads, at the approach of frost may be taken up and thickly planted in a forcing-pit, under sashes. Here, by watering, airing, and good attention, good heads may be had until mid-winter.

Marketing.—Cauliflowers are sent from here to New York by railroad, and generally packed in barrels, but I believe latticed boxes of moderate and uniform size would be preferable. It is advisable to have them as large and fully developed as possible, and yet avoid letting them burst out or start to seed.

They should be cut the same as a head of early cabbage, and the outer leaves trimmed off evenly, nearly or quite down to the head, that the latter may be completely exposed, and pack so that they may not get bruised.

Seed.—The seed is mainly procured from Europe, and there is but little grown in this country, from the fact that our summers are too hot for it.

If planted very early it will blossom, and some seed will set under favorable circumstances, but the surest way is to sow in July, transplant, and keep the partially-grown heads over winter in a cold-frame or cellar, and set them out early in the spring, something similar to our treatment of early cabbages for the same purpose.

Varieties.—The Early Erfurt and Early Paris are used for first crop; the Nonpareil and Half-early Paris for succession, and the Le Normand and Walcheren for late.

CARROT.

This is somewhat extensively grown by market-gardeners, and is a valuable crop for the farm-gardener as well, as it can be shipped to distant markets, and besides is very useful for feeding, especially for horses and colts, being somewhat laxative, assisting digestion, promoting healthfulness, and adding much to the appearance of the animal. The demand for carrots in cities for feeding purposes is yearly increasing, and they bring remunerative prices. In view of these facts, considering the comparative ease with which they can be grown, too much value can not be placed on this crop.

Soil and Preparation.—The carrot succeeds best in a loamy soil, rather light than otherwise, and may be grown in such as is generally termed sandy land. It does not require over-rich soil, and will do full as well on land well manured the previous year as when the manure is applied at the time of sowing. Twenty two-horse loads of stable-manure to the acre, broadcast, plowed in, or one thousand pounds of bone-flour, or five hundred pounds of guano, harrowed in, will, in naturally good soil, be sufficient. The land should be deeply plowed, finely and thoroughly harrowed, smoothed with the back of the harrow, and if not then free from lumps raked by hand.

Sowing and Cultivating.—The seed should be sown immediately after the land is prepared, that it may come in contact with the natural moisture, and the more readily germinate. For garden culture the rows should be marked out fifteen inches apart, one and a half inch deep, and the entire working done by hand, but where land is plenty they may be double that distance, and worked with a cultivator. In the former case the seed should be sown quite thick, and covered by raking in. As soon as the rows can be traced, use a push-hoe, cutting close to the plants, and when nicely up, they must be thinned to three inches apart, and, of course, all weeds removed from the rows ; a fortnight after the soil should be loosened by deep hoeing, and later the push-hoe may be used, and such weeds in the rows as were previously overlooked be pulled by hand. In the latter case they are seldom thinned, except by occasionally cutting out a bunch with one corner of the hoe, and by this plan the seed must be thinly sown, and great pains taken in preparing the soil and covering the seed, lest it will not come up even. I would advise in either case that the seed be sown thick (as the germ is weak, and does not always come up well when sown thin), and afterwards thinned by hand, leaving the plants equi-distant, by which means, when harvested, the roots will be more uniform in size, and the crop enough heavier to repay the extra labor. When grown wide the push-hoe may be used to advantage along the rows before the plants are large enough to admit using the cultivator. All subsequent working can be done by horse and hoe, twice going over being sufficient in clean land; and I would here add, that crops of this kind should never be sown where foul seed and weeds abound. For early, the seed may be sown as soon as the ground can be worked in the spring, and for main crop any time until July.

Gardeners generally sow in May, following a crop of spinach, sprouts, radishes, etc. From two to four pounds of seed will be required to an acre, according to the distance between the rows.

Preparing for Market.—Early-sown carrots are pulled when half-grown, trimmed, washed, and tied in flat bunches of from four to six.

The main crop is sold by the barrel, and the only preparation necessary is to remove all fibrous roots, and when they have been stored, the sprouts must be cut off, and retail dealers prefer to have them washed. When sold for feeding or shipping to a distance, they must be dry, as they will keep much better.

Gathering and Storing.—The roots can be taken up with a spade, but the quickest plan is to run a plow deeply beside the row, and, placing the spade back of the row, they can be quite easily pried out. Whether for marketing or for seed the method of storing is the same, and should be done according to directions given in the chapter on storing for winter.

The general treatment is the same as for beets, except that the tops can be cut off to better advantage than by twisting—the same care is necessary to avoid cutting the hearts, when the roots are intended for seed. The middle of November is quite as late as the crop can with safety be left in the ground, although the roots will not be materially injured by light freezing before they are taken out.

Seed.—Pains must be taken to make selections for seed, true to the variety, which may be done as directed for beets. The seed does best in a rather strong loam, moderately rich. After plowing and harrowing, make rows three feet apart with the marker, along which with a crowbar make holes eighteen inches apart; place the roots therein, the crowns level with the surface, fastening the earth firmly against them with a dibble. They should be set out about the middle of April or as soon as all danger of very severe freezing is past.

The after-culture is the same as for beets, except that ridging is unnecessary, and the same plan of planting every fifth row with potatoes will facilitate the gathering of the seed. The seeds are produced in heads or clusters at the extremities of the branches, and ripen unevenly, hence they require repeated cuttings. When ripe, which may be known by the seed changing to a brown color and the branches commencing to dry, the heads must be cut with shears, gathered into a barrel, carried to the loft, and spread over the floor. When the crop has all been gathered and the whole become thoroughly dry, the heads can be removed to the thrashing floor, and thrashed with a flail, only hard enough to separate the seed from the small sticks which support them, and avoid as much as possible breaking these sticks, in order to make the cleaning more easy. When thrashed, separate the coarser sticks from the seed with a No. 4, and again with a No. 6 sieve, rubbing the larger seeds through with the hand; place the seed thinly on a large cloth, exposed to the sun, and after it has lain so for five or six hours, set a barrel in the center; on this place a No. 8 sieve, through which pass the seed by rubbing with the hand, throwing out the sticks as they accumulate in the sieve. Repeat this operation the following day, this time using No. 10 sieve, which will remove the furze or beard, when it may be finally cleaned by passing twice through the fan-mill, and finished by No. 24 sieve. But a very few years ago it was believed that the removal of the furze injured the seed, and it was carefully picked out by hand, but experience has proved to the contrary, and now not a pound of seed is sold in any seed store in this country but that which is rubbed clean, in which condition it is more easily handled and can be more easily and evenly sown.

Carrot seed retains its vitality two years.

Varieties.—There are but two distinct varieties much grown for marketing.

Early Horn.—This is grown principally for early bunching. For main crop, in very shallow soils, it could be grown to better advantage than the long varieties, though it would not be so salable, except for feeding purposes. Root about six inches long, quite thick, and tapering abruptly at the bottom; skin and flesh orange yellow; foliage small.

Long Orange.—This is the universal favorite in this country for marketing or feeding. Root long and tapering; skin and flesh orange-yellow; foliage strong.

CELERY.

This with market-gardeners—especially those about New York—is one of the main crops, and hundreds of thousands of roots are annually grown. It is not a very good article for shipping as usually prepared for market, but considerable quantities are shipped as taken from the ground.

Soil and Preparation.—Celery will do well in any soil between sand and clay, provided it is made very rich and thoroughly worked.

It is grown by market-gardeners as a second crop, after cabbages, onions, etc., which are always very heavily manured in the spring, and enough manure is left in the soil to bring through the crop of celery, so that it is planted without further manuring; and in fact, applications of manure immediately preceding this crop have a tendency to cause the leaves to rust, damaging and even destroying the celery for marketing. The method of growing celery at the present time is greatly simplified over the old style. Then, deep trenches were dug out, manure spaded in, and much labor bestowed, uselessly, as a comparison with the modern plan will show. After the first crop is removed, the land should be cleared of all weeds and refuse, deeply plowed, harrowed fine, and smoothed off, and rows made with the marker three feet apart for the dwarf, and four feet for the larger kinds. These rows should be sunk an inch or two, and made even by the face of a hoe-blade drawn along, thus leaving a broad and level surface to receive the plants.

This preparation, as in the case of land for late cabbages, must be made in anticipation of rain, as the transplanting is done at midsummer, when it not unfrequently happens there is but little weather suited to this work; hence, everything must be in readiness to take advantage of the first shower.

Sowing Seed and Growing Plants.—The seed may be sown in a hot-bed or cold-frame, if plants are desired early, but for main crop it must be sown in the open air, as early in the spring as the ground can be worked. Select a piece of rich, mellow soil, a little moist than otherwise; plow a bed four to six feet wide, and any length required; spade this over, mixing in fine well-rotted manure; make the soil fine, rake with a steel rake, making the surface level and entirely free from lumps or stones.

In sowing, use a board eight or nine inches broad, and as long as the bed is wide; lay the board across the bed, and with a small stick or the point of a dibble make a shallow mark on each side of it, in which deposit the seed with the thumb and finger, thinly and evenly; turn the board over twice, again mark and sow, and so proceed until the bed is sown; then from each side, reaching half-way over the bed, draw the back of a spade over each row, at the same time pressing the soil; and this is all the covering required.

If the weather is dry an occasional watering at evening will be beneficial.

An ounce of seed will produce six thousand plants. As soon as the plants appear, carefully hoe them, and remove all weeds from the rows; twice hoeing and weeding will usually suffice, but do not allow the weeds to get the least start. Should the plants be large enough to set out before the ground is ready to receive them, the tops may be shorn off, which will make them stouter and prevent them from growing spindling.

Planting and Cultivating.—During the month of July;

when the weather is suitable, the plants should be set out six inches apart in the rows with a dibble, pressing the earth firmly to the roots, and carefully avoid burying the hearts. For an acre, about twenty-nine thousand plants are required at three feet, and about twenty-two thousand at four feet, between the rows. The plants must be carefully pulled from the bed, held evenly in one hand until it is full, when the points of the roots and the tops of the leaves should be cut off.

The object of this is to stiffen the root, making the work of transplanting the more rapid, and causing the young rootlets to form quicker, and by trimming the leaves they do not wilt and fall over so easily as when whole. The outer leaves eventually die away, as new ones are formed from the heart. To facilitate operations, one man or a stout boy should be in advance of the planters with a basket of plants, handing them out as they are wanted, and another should pull and prepare the plants. When transplanted in partially moist ground, as after a light shower, it is advisable to "puddle" the roots as directed in the chapter on transplanting. In a few days the plants will have taken root, when the earth may be stirred by a fine rake, drawing it diagonally from the rows, thus not only loosening the soil, but destroying one crop of weeds, the seeds of which will have already started. A week or so later, the push-hoe may be run on each side of the rows, and the earth between stirred by the harrow-toothed cultivator. When the plants get fairly started, the broad-toothed cultivator may be used, and the ground around the plants worked with a hoe, removing all weeds.

The growing of celery is at a season when the weed known as "purslane" grows rapidly, and if this once gets a start, it will be almost impossible to check it; hence, keeping the ground constantly stirred is of great importance. As the plants advance in growth, the earth

4*

must be gradually drawn to them, and when they are about twelve or fifteen inches high, a light furrow can be thrown toward them on each side preparatory to "handling." This is done by firmly grasping the leaves in one hand, and drawing the fine soil to them with the other, pressing it against the plant, being careful always not to allow the earth to come in contact with the heart. Follow with the hoe, and draw the fine earth well around the plants. This operation causes the plants to grow upright and straight, which is of importance when they come to be stored. When celery is grown early for using in the fall, the same cultivation is required, and in addition "banking" must be performed. This follows the earthing-up last described as soon as the leaves have grown out and commenced spreading again. It must be done when the soil is moist enough to compact readily.

With a spade, cut away the earth nearly perpendicularly about twelve or fifteen inches from the plants, throwing up the soil against the plants, catching it by quickly turning the spade, and pressing it firmly. The sides may thus be run up or "banked" at intervals, as the leaves grow, working the soil about the leaves by the hand, and gently pressing until the plants have grown to full length, or are sufficiently "blanched" below to be fit to use.

This is virtually overground trenching, and serves to whiten or "blanch" the leaves. Trenching, though once extensively practised, is now only used to a limited extent among market-gardeners, and to produce a small quantity early. In growing for seed, the same cultivation is necessary as for market, except that as the roots have to be kept late the following spring, they may be planted as late as the first of August, and not blanched, but merely worked up enough to make the stalks upright.

Preparing for Market.—That which has been "banked

up" and that "earthed up" pretty high will be marketable during the fall or early winter.

The earth must be removed, the plants carefully lifted with a spade, and carried to the "market-house."

Remove the outer leaves, and on one side of the plant break them away sufficiently to well expose the heart.

Cut away the small roots, and square the main root, leaving the end rather thick, the better to hold the string; wash with a soft brush, having long bristles at the ends, so as to work well in among the leaves. In tying, select the requisite number of roots for a bunch—from three to six; usually four in the fall, and five late in the winter; lay them out to form a good-shaped bunch, always keeping uppermost that side of each root which has the heart most exposed. Tie a string firmly around the root of one, then around the next, and so on until the whole are tied together; trim the points of the roots even, grasp the leaves in the hand, and around them near the tips tie a string, always bending the outer leaves to give the bunch a spreading appearance. Place one dozen in a pile, for convenience in handling. The best of the outer leaves, and in winter such roots as are not large enough for flat bunching, may be tied in round bunches, and are usually sold under the name of "soup-celery." Celery which has been stored should be prepared in the manner above described, but generally more roots will be required for a bunch, and the bunches will not make so nice an appearance unless unusually well kept, but it is more thoroughly blanched and more eatable, and consequently in greater demand, especially about the holidays.

In sending to market, it should be well protected in cold weather, as freezing after blanching will destroy the color and damage the sale.

Market-gardeners generally use large boxes lined with straw mats, and covered with sail-cloth, in which they place the celery to be conveyed to market,

Storing for Market.—Celery will not be injured by light frosts, but heavy freezing is very injurious, and it is well to begin the storing of this crop in good season. About the first of November the first may be put away, and small lots at intervals, completing the whole by the first of December. The object of this is to have it marketable in succession, the first stored usually being the first blanched, and so on. Celery in storing should only be handled when dry, and never put away while it is frozen. It sometimes happens at the season for storing that the nights are very frosty, thus preventing handling *early* the following day. To overcome this, dig the roots in the afternoon; stack them along the trench, tops outside, and cover with mats or cloths, and they may be put in the trenches as early as convenient the next morning.

Dig a trench the width of the spade as deep as the celery is high, and any length required; run a plow on each side of the rows, and with a spade carefully lift the plants; place them perpendicularly in the trench, stowing them compactly; afterwards, at intervals, press fine earth down beside and up to the tops of the leaves, and by cold weather have the whole ridge formed, the more readily to carry away the water. The covering of the trench should be gradual, to prevent heating, but when complete and the ground is frozen over, put on sufficient coarse manure to prevent severe freezing; this can be readily removed, and the roots quite easily taken out when wanted.

Seed.—Selections should be made according to the peculiar points of the variety, the object being to secure such as are perfectly solid in the stems, and with an abundance of solid heart-leaves.

The storing is the same as when designed for market, but as it must be kept until quite late in the spring it is an object to keep it dry, and this can be done in a great measure by nailing common boards together in the shape of a V, and inverting them over the trench, forming a roof, and covering the whole with manure. It is advisable to store celery for seed in very dry soil. The chances, even at the best, are that many which may appear sound in the spring, will decay when transplanted; hence it is advisable to bed them quite thickly in a cold-frame as soon as one can be spared. They must here be partially shaded for a few days, gradually hardened off, though not allowed to freeze, and about the first of May such as prove sound should be planted out.

Use good land for growing celery seed. Plow and harrow well, giving a liberal dressing of well-rotted stable-manure, unless the soil is already very rich. Mark out light furrows four feet apart; with a trowel set the roots eighteen inches apart in the rows, pressing the earth about the root, but leaving the heart exposed; keep free from weeds by the use of the cultivator and hoe, and at the last working slightly ridge about the plants. Celery produces seed quite profusely, in small clusters, at the ends of the very numerous small twigs which grow out from the stalk and branches. It ripens very irregularly, an individual stalk often containing blossoms and green and ripe seed at the same time; hence, some judgment is required in cutting it.

When the bulk of seed on a plant is ripe, which may be known by the brown color, the stalk should be cut at the root, and all such removed on cloths and lightly thrashed at once, which will remove all dead-ripe seed; the stalks must then be laid on shutters and exposed to the sun for two days, and again thrashed, when all seed that is sufficiently ripe to germinate will readily fall from the stalks. The seed must be spread thin, on cloths, in a loft, for ten days or more, when it can be run twice through the fan-mill and finally cleaned by the No. 24 sieve.

Celery seed retains its vitality five years.

Varieties.—The distinct varieties of celery in common cultivation are very few; many gardeners claim to have a variety of their own which is designated by the name of the proprietor, in general parlance, as Brown's kind, Smith's kind, etc., as the case may be, but in these there is but little if any difference.

The main points of celery for market are stout heads, solid leaf-stalks, and abundant heart. The tall-growing varieties are now but little cultivated, the dwarf being preferred, from the fact that it can be grown more closely together, and is easier worked than the former.

Giant White Solid.—Leaves not very abundant; heart-leaves long and solid; hight three feet.

A few years since this was the standard sort among market-gardeners.

Dwarf White Solid.—Leaves abundant; hearts profuse and solid; about two feet in hight and very stout. Now generally in use among market-gardeners, and grown under various names, as previously stated.

Dwarf Red Solid.—Very similar to the above, except as to color, the stalk of the leaves being purplish red, and when blanched the hearts are marked with rosy pink, presenting a very rich appearance. In my opinion decidedly the finest flavored, and generally the best of all.

CORN.

Sweet corn, or that used in the green state for the table, is not grown much by market-gardeners, but is quite an important crop with farm-gardeners not far distant from city markets. If carefully packed it may be shipped to a distance to advantage.

Soil and Preparation.—Sweet corn should have rather light soil, and as it is very important to get it early into market, it should be planted in land which can be worked early, and lies well to the sun. As the crop will be off in time to allow turnips to be sown, it will be well to manure quite heavily for this crop, in anticipation of the second one. Apply twenty two-horse loads of stable manure, plowed in, or one thousand pounds of bone-flour, or five hundred pounds of guano, harrowed in, to the acre. Mark out furrows four feet apart; put in some well-rotted manure or compost, with which mix a little soil; drop the seed from three to six inches apart, cover two inches deep, and press with the hoe. When desirable to work both ways with a horse, mark furrows, three and a half feet apart each way, and at the angles place a half-shovelful of manure, mixing some soil with it, and put in six or eight kernels to each hill; cover with two inches of fine earth, and press firmly with the hoe-blade. About one peck of seed will be required for an acre.

The amount of seed in the row or hill must be in accordance with the season, and if planted early—which it always should be for first crop, even at the risk of having to replant—it must be put in quite thick, as in all probability some will rot. When fairly above ground cultivate and hoe, and when all danger of frost is past, thin to one foot apart in the rows, or four to a hill. The usual time for planting is the first of May, but if it can be got in earlier all the better, if the land lies warm. It may be planted for succession at intervals until July.

Marketing.—The fitness of corn for the table, and hence for market, can be determined by the kernels filling out plump and entirely covering the cob, but as the husking to inspect its condition damages the looks, and by exposing the kernels would spoil the whole, growers pull the ears in accordance with the appearance of the silk which protrudes from the ends, as well as by feeling. To understand the proper condition of the silk can only be acquired by experience, and to learn this a few ears must be husked at various stages. Suffice it to say no corn is fit to market while the silk, or at least so much of it as protrudes from the husks, is green. Sweet corn can be shipped in bulk, but it is more convenient to place it promiscuously in well-ventilated barrels.

Seed.—Sweet corn will mix with field corn if grown near it; hence, to keep the stock pure, this must be avoided. The cultivation is the same as for market, and should be planted about the middle of May. Good sweet corn for seed can be grown on inverted sward-land, using as a fertilizer a handful of bone-phosphate to each hill, well mixed with the soil. When the stalks begin to dry they must be cut and bound in small shocks, the same as field corn, and afterwards the ears husked out and spread in a loft to dry thoroughly. The nicest but the most laborious way to save seed sweet-corn is, when the stalks are partially dry, to break the whole ear off, and with one or two of the outer husks, tie six or eight ears together, and hang them over a fence or in a loft until they become perfectly dry, when they may be husked out. The small grains at the point of the ear and all imperfect grains should be removed, the balance shelled by hand and passed through the fan-mill. Sweet corn retains moisture a long time, and must not be hastily stored away in bulk. If kept from the weevil it retains its vitality two years.

Varieties.—The varieties are numerous, but those in general cultivation are few.

Extra Early Dwarf Sugar.—The earliest known sort; stalk three and a half to four feet high; ears short, eight-rowed, rather small for market; valuable for its earliness.

Early Eight-rowed Sugar.—The best early variety to grow for market in quantity; stalk five feet high; ears eight-rowed; about eight inches long, tapering to the point; kernels plump and full.

Mammoth or Excelsior Sweet.—The best of all sweet corn, but rather late; stalk six feet; ears twelve to sixteen rows, eight to twelve inches long, thick at the point; kernels long and slender, very much indented.

CUCUMBERS.

These can be safely shipped a long distance, and hence are worthy the attention of those who are remote from market, and desire to grow vegetables for profit.

Soil and Preparation.—The soil best adapted to cucumbers is a sandy loam, and they will do well on very sandy land if an abundance of manure is applied. Where manure can be obtained it is far preferable to plow under a good dressing, as the vines are rank feeders. As a rule they are grown in hills.

For this plan, plow and harrow the ground, furrow out six feet for the large, or four and a half feet for the small-growing kinds, one way, and three feet the other. At every crossing put a shovelful of well-rotted manure or compost and thoroughly mix it with the soil.

Planting and Cultivating.—The season for planting is from the first to the tenth of May for early, and at any time thence until the first of July, at which latter date those designed for pickles may be planted, their after-cultivation being the same as when the crop is to be full-grown. When the manure can be put in broadcast, mark light furrows five to seven feet apart, according to the kind to be planted; long varieties make the most vine, and *vice versa*.

Drop in the seed thickly, certainly twelve or fifteen to a foot, which will allow a fair share for the "striped bug," which is certain to give them a call. Cover an inch deep with fine soil, and press with the hoe-blade. When grown in hills, about twenty seeds should be placed in each, and covered as in rows.

As soon as the young plants begin to break through,

the bugs must be looked after. I have known them to eat off the plant before it was fairly out of the ground, and if attention is given to them at this time, the crop may be saved, or if passed by for a day or two the whole may be destroyed. Tobacco-dust, bone-flour, ashes, etc., are recommended to destroy or drive away these pests, but I have always found *air-slaked shell-lime* to be the most effectual. It is quite essential to procure a barrel or two of burnt oyster-shells in early spring, and put them into a box or cask large enough to allow of nearly double increase of bulk by slaking. The lime should be kept in a dry place, exposed to the air, by the action of which it will in time slake, and crumble fine. This should be sifted as wanted, and the *dust* sprinkled over and under the young plants, even before a bug may be seen, as with these "an ounce of prevention is worth a pound of cure." As the plants grow they should be limed every few days, until they begin to run, applying the dust *very early* in the morning while the dew is on, thus causing it to adhere, throwing it well under as well as sprinkling it over the plants. When the plants are nicely up work with the cultivator and hoe, and repeat it as often as possible, for working among the plants disturbs the bugs, as well as loosens the soil and destroys the weeds. When the plants begin to run or form a vine they must be thinned out to twelve inches if in rows, or three plants may be left in a hill. If just after this they receive a thorough cultivating and hoeing, they will scarcely require any more attention, as the vines will soon cover the ground. Cucumbers may be advanced by starting them under glass in a cold-frame about the first of May. Cut sods about three inches thick, and in pieces four inches square; lay them up-side down on the level surface of the cold-bed; after taking out an inch or more of the soil from the center of each sod, drop in a few seeds and cover with fine earth; water, and place on the sashes. In a few days they will have started, when they will require airing every mild day and closing at night. There is but little danger of bugs when grown this way, and by the twentieth of the month they may be removed to the open air, provided the weather is settled. Of course the sod is to be lifted with the plants, and when set out, if they show any signs of wilting, give a good watering at evening. When firmly established they must be thinned to three plants in a hill, the preparation of the soil and after-treatment being the same as for regular out-door culture. When it is desired to force cucumbers, after the crop of cabbage or other plants has been removed from the cold-frames, always by the first of May, the soil should be spaded and raked, and a few seeds planted in the center of each section, or immediately under the center of each sash.

The sashes being placed on, the seeds will soon germinate, and when strong, thin to three to a sash.

In this case the plants may be forced somewhat by keeping pretty close, but avoid excessive heat, as it will weaken them, or they may be scorched, to their injury. At the same time guard against sudden changes to cold, when the sashes are opened.

When the weather becomes warm and the vines require room, the sashes may be entirely removed.

Marketing.—Cucumbers should always be cut, never pulled, as that disturbs and injures the vines. They are ready for market when a little more than half-grown, or while they still retain their green color. When grown near a market, washing will improve their appearance, but for shipping they are better if left dry, but avoid having them wilted. They may be shipped in barrels or boxes, but should not be long packed in bulk. Pickles must be cut when one fourth to one half grown, and these, as well as when grown full size, will be increased in number by keeping them cut clean, for when a part is allowed to ripen but few more set, and the vines soon die.

Seed.—When grown for seed the same course must be pursued as when grown for market, except that they need not be planted until near the first of June. To insure a large crop, the first setting must be cut when young, and the second blossoms will yield more than twofold. Some advise pinching the ends of the young vines to produce fruitfulness, but I have never seen any benefit from it. With pure stock there is but little choice in selecting. A few of the very best may be taken for stock seed, but when properly grown the whole crop will be even and uniform. When the fruit is ripe, which may be known by their changing color from green to white or yellow, according to the variety, they must be gathered into a barn or shed to be cut. This is work which may be done on wet or stormy days, but it is not advisable to let the cucumbers remain long in a heap, for they will soon rot after removal from the vines, which makes dirty work, and causes some loss of seed. The cucumbers must be cut lengthwise, and the seeds scraped out by the thumb and fingers into a tub, from whence they must be emptied into tight barrels to sour, in order to remove the mucilaginous pulp in which each seed is encased. The barrels must not be more than three fourths full, for in course of fermentation the mass increases in bulk nearly one fourth, for which this allowance must be made.

The whole should be thoroughly stirred at least once every day, and will be ready for washing in about five days, or when the seed all settles to the bottom, though it may remain longer without injury if solely in the natural juice. The washing must be done on a clear day, and commenced early in the morning, that the seed may become partially dry by night. Take a large tub (usually a half-hogshead), fill it two thirds with water, and pass the seed through a No. 3 sieve, into the water; the sieve should be held partially under, and worked about in the water; this will retain any pieces of skin or coarse matter in the sieve, and the seeds will settle to the bottom. Not more than one barrel of pulp can be conveniently washed at one time, and each lot of seed will require several waters, which will carry away the pulp in pouring off, and eventually leave the seed clean in the bottom of the tub.

The seed must be taken out in sieves Nos. 8 and 10, and left to drain while another lot is being washed, when it must be placed on shutters, such as are used on coldframes, in the sun, to dry; the second lot taken out, and so on, until the whole is complete. The next day the seed can be placed thin on cloths, again exposed to the sun; afterwards removed to a loft, and kept spread thin on cloths until perfectly dry, when it may be passed through the fan-mill, and finally cleaned by No. 10 sieve, which will remove the sand, and it can then be stored.

The seed retains its vitality more than ten years.

Varieties.—The difference in the leading varieties is quite marked.

They readily mix with each other and with melons, and other vegetables of their class, and consequently all such must in cultivation be kept widely separated to preserve them pure.

Early Russian.—The earliest and smallest of all. Fruit pale green, when ripe brownish yellow; seldom three inches in length, thick, and blunt at the ends; usually produced in pairs; plants small, and very productive. Like all short varieties a free seeder, and I may here remark that the larger and longer the cucumber, the less seed is produced in proportion.

Early Cluster.—An old and favorite variety. Fruit dark green above, pale below and at the ends; when ripe dark yellow or orange; about six inches in length, thick, tapering at the stem, rather blunt at the blossom-end; grows in clusters; plants not of the largest, but free growers in good soil; very productive; a free seeder. A valuable variety for pickles.

Early White-Spine.—The general favorite about New York for marketing. Fruit glossy green, growing lighter by age, and when ripe nearly or quite white; prickles white, distinct from most other varieties, eight to ten inches in length, rather thin in comparison with the cluster, and tapering at the stem-end; plants remarkably free growers, and very productive; a moderate seeder.

London Long Green.—Fruit dark green; when ripe brownish yellow, about twelve inches in length, tapering at the stem; plants not very free growers, not productive, and a shy seeder.

EGG-PLANT.

A native of a tropical climate, extremely sensitive to cold, and consequently quite difficult to grow. The fruit can be readily shipped, but requires careful handling, as the skin is quite easily disfigured, and the appearance is much damaged when bruised. On account of the attention required in the early stages, they are not extensively cultivated. The demand for them is steadily increasing, and where the climate suits they may be profitably grown. They succeed best during very hot, dry weather; and when it happens there is much rain about the time of blossoming, but few fruit will set.

Sowing Seed and Growing the Plants.—The seed should be sown in a hot-bed, and requires more heat than any other to germinate it.

If sown the first of April, the plants may be sufficiently forwarded to give a crop for market, but as I have always grown them for seed purposes specially, and the fruit requiring at least one month after it is eatable to perfect the seed, I find it necessary to sow by the first of March. It is true we have much extra labor in guarding the plants one month more at a very inclement season of the year, and also the trouble and expense of making an extra hot-bed, but this is more than compensated by the returns from a full crop of seed. In either case, the hot-bed should be made as directed under that head, with an addition of six inches more of manure. The surface must be raked even, and enough sifted soil be added to make the depth six inches, when the plants are to remain in the seed-bed until transplanted to the open ground; but three inches will be sufficient when it is designed to use a second hot-bed. Spread the seed even and thin; one ounce of seed will sow two sashes, and produce two thousand plants; cover with one half an inch of very fine soil; water lightly from a fine-rose watering-pot; put on the sashes, and cover the whole from the sun for twenty-four hours; then remove the shading, and allow the vapor to pass away, but do not allow the bed to become chilled, by opening each end-sash one inch from the top for a short time in the middle of the day. The bed must not be allowed to become dry, nor yet be kept very wet; the upper part may need an occasional sprinkling, but the lower half will be naturally moist enough. When the plants first come up, they are very liable to damp off, and at this time but little water must be used—the vapor must be allowed to pass off; still beware of chilling the plants. If sown the first of April, the plants may be thinned to four inches apart; but when sown the first of March, I prepare a second and larger hot-bed when the plants are forming the second leaves, which is tempered and ready by the time the plants are large enough to handle easily.

In this bed the soil is at least six inches deep, raked fine, and the surface even. In this the young plants are pricked out six inches apart, lightly watered, the sashes put on, the plants shaded for a day or two, and during the middle of the day for two or three days longer. Egg-plants have but few fibrous roots, consequently they are difficult to transplant, and great care must be taken to press the earth against the root, and to properly attend to the shading. Water can only be used sparingly, for until the plants again become established there is danger of damping off. They now require regular airing, and by good attention, with the fresh heat under them, they soon outgrow those in the seed-bed, and at the season of transplanting, from the twentieth of May to the first of June, we have large, strong plants to set out. As the plants advance in growth, the frames must be raised and blocked up, so that the leaves do not touch the glass—an advantage in movable frames—and before setting out, the sashes must be removed to harden the plants. Weeds will grow freely among the plants, and must be regularly pulled out, and the surface occasionally stirred by the finger.

Soil, Planting, and Cultivation.—Egg-plants require a deep, light, warm soil, and it can hardly be made too rich. The land may be prepared about the middle of May in readiness for planting, which is usually done about the twenty-fifth, a rainy day or just after a rain being the most suitable time.

Apply a liberal quantity of stable-manure or bone-dust, plow deep, and harrow thoroughly; mark out furrows four feet apart, in which place a shovelful of well-rotted manure or compost every three feet, and thoroughly mix it into the soil with a hoe, forming a slight hill with a concave center six or eight inches in depth.

When the weather is suitable for transplanting, water the bed *copiously*, thoroughly saturating the soil; lift the plants by means of a trowel, securing large balls of earth to the roots, and remove them in wheelbarrows to the place of planting. Set the plants in the holes, drawing the earth to them, and firmly pressing it about the root with the hands. Those grown in the seed-bed, if properly thinned, may be removed the same way, which is far preferable to lifting without the earth attached.

The after-cultivation consists only in keeping the ground free from weeds, which is readily done by the cultivator and hoe.

Cutting for Market.—The fruit is marketable when about half-grown, usually six to eight inches long, and five to six inches in diameter at the thickest part. This, however, can only be determined by some experience with them. They are not eatable when the seeds begin to swell, which may be known by the color of the fruit changing from bright to dull purple.

On account of the thorns on the stems of some, they are most easily cut with a strong pair of shears.

They should not be washed, but may be wiped off and carefully laid in barrels for shipping.

Seed.—To keep up and improve the variety, such as are wanted for stock seed should be selected when growing, and marked by crossing with a knife. For this purpose select the earliest, best formed, and particularly the deepest colored, and as far as possible from productive plants. Some may prefer to select those without thorns on the stem, as these are pleasanter to handle, but I have found the thorny-stemmed ones the most productive, and the fruit is more handsome than that from the smooth-stemmed.

The latter are, however, a little earlier than the former, so that one thing balances the other, and it is quite as well to grow them promiscuously. When the fruit is ripe, which may be known by the change from bright purple to dull purple, and sometimes to a deep yellow, those marked for stock must first be gathered, and it is recommended in selecting from the marked fruit to take only such as have held their color well toward maturity. It is advisable to make two or three gatherings of the main crop, as the first ripe are liable to rot before the later ones are fit for seed. At the first frost all that are marketable may be cut and sold, as they will not ripen the seed. Cut with shears, cart to the shed or barn, and prepare for mashing or grinding. The primitive mode, which must yet be resorted to where machinery is not at command, is to cut away one third or more of the fruit from the stem-end, and peel the skin from the balance. It will be observed that there are no seeds in the upper or stem-end and those below lie over one fourth of an inch from the skin; hence much may be cut away to reduce the labor of mashing or grinding as well as washing. The peeled fruit may be placed in small quantity in a strong barrel, and mashed to a fine pulp, emptied into other barrels, and this continued until finished, or they may be ground in a portable cider or wine mill. I have always used Krauser's Patent Portable Cider-Mill, for these and all other things which require to be ground up in order to procure the seed. This mill has two reciprocating levers working alternately against a rough cylinder, and by placing the cut part against the cylinder, bottom-end down, the pulp is scooped out, and the skins which pass through whole are quickly taken out in washing. To prepare the fruit for this mill we simply cut away the top and quarter the other part, and for mashing by hand or grinding in other mills they should also be cut, as well as peeled. In cutting avoid using a very sharp knife, lest many seeds be cut and spoiled, and after the fruits are cut they must be ground immediately, for they quickly heat and rot. The pulp, to work nicely, should be washed the day after grinding, but may remain longer without injury to the seed.

The washing is done principally in the same manner as cucumber seed, except that we use a No. 3 sieve first, and as each lot receives its third washing the seed is removed to a barrel, and when the whole is thus far cleaned it is again washed as before, using sieve No. 6. Two or three changes of water will make the seed perfectly free from pulp, when it must be taken out in sieves Nos. 12 and 14, drained, and spread thinly on shutters. Egg-plant seed is very liable to sprout after washing unless quickly dried; hence it is very important to select a dry day for the operation, and to commence early in the morning, so as to get the seed out before noon, between which time and night, if spread thin, exposed to the sun, and frequently stirred, it will be fit to put on cloths, and be removed to a loft, where it may be left spread thin until thoroughly dry. It may afterwards be cleaned by passing through the wind, or large lots through the fan-mill, and the sand removed by sieve No. 12. The seed, when well kept, retains its vitality five years.

Varieties.—The varieties are not numerous, and the older sorts are known as "Long Purple" and "Round Purple," differing mainly in the shape of the fruit.

The general favorite at the present time is the

New York Improved Large Purple.—This is an improvement on the "Round Purple" made by carefully selecting the fruit for a succession of years. It was grown by my father while gardening at Jersey City. He annually took the first premium at the American Institute Fairs, which fact excited the attention of a New York seedsman, who contracted with him for an annual supply of seed, and gave it the name it still bears.

Plant upright and compact; fruit, when marketable, six to nine inches in length, and four to six inches in diameter, thinnest at the stem, sometimes indented or grooved on one side; color bright velvety purple, changing to dull purple and yellow when ripe, at which stage it frequently attains a size of twelve inches in length and eight inches in diameter; stems quite thickly covered with thorns on many of the plants.

Black Pekin.—A very distinct variety, quite recently introduced. Plant large and branching, with purple stalks; the leaves green, distinctly marked with purple and bronzed; very ornamental; fruit of medium size, rarely over six inches in diameter, nearly round; color black-purple, which it retains until maturity. Its fitness for seed is determined by shrinking of the skin when ripe.

HERBS.

The cultivation of the leading herbs is a business of some magnitude with market-gardeners, and worthy the attention of those who are remote from market, for in the dry state they may be packed without risk, and shipped any distance, and they will not be damaged if lightly packed when green, provided they are not kept so long enough to heat. Such as are generally grown are here described. All herbs require a light rich soil, which should be made fine on the surface, and generally well prepared. They may be grown as second crops when intended for market, by sowing in April and transplanting to the first cleared ground. What is generally termed a bunch is about one half as much as can be spanned by the thumb and forefinger. This must be firmly bound at the bottom, and usually two bunches are connected for convenience in hanging up to dry.

Sage.—Mark rows one inch deep and fifteen inches apart, in which deposit the seed moderately thin, covering with a rake, gently pressing the earth. The young plants may be set out fifteen inches apart, or they may be thinned and left to grow where sown. The plants usually survive the winter, and may be parted and reset every spring, which is the better plan in growing for seed. The stems should be gathered just before blossoming, and the crop may be cut twice in one season if grown early.

It will generally give a fair yield of marketable leaves after the seed has been cut. The seed is produced in open cups on slender branches, growing above the leaves, and when ripe, which may be known by its changing to black, the branches must be cut and placed on cloths, until the whole is collected, as it ripens unevenly and requires frequent cuttings. When dry it will readily thrash out, and can be easily cleaned with Nos. 6 and 12 sieves, with the aid of a gentle breeze.

The only variety cultivated for market is known as the "Broad-leaved."

Sweet Marjoram.—This should be sown in the latter part of April, the same way precisely as directed for Celery. The young plants must be kept clean by repeated light hoeing and weeding, and when large enough to handle nicely be transplanted twelve inches apart each way, leaving some to grow in the seed-bed. This will not survive our winters, hence must be sown every year. It must be cut when in bloom. The seed is produced within a "button" of small scales, very similar in appearance to hops, and when ripe, which may be known by the leaves and buttons commencing to dry, the stems may be cut entire, and as the seed is extremely small, must be kept on cloths of very fine texture.

It can be quite easily thrashed and rubbed out when dry, and cleaned with sieves Nos. 14, 20, and 40, and a very gentle breeze. The variety known as "Knotted Marjoram" is the only one of any importance.

Summer Savory.—Sow the first of May, in the manner of Sage, in very shallow drills; thin, as this must not be transplanted, but allowed to grow in the seed bed.

The cutting for market and also saving the seed is the same as directed for Sweet Marjoram, using sieves Nos. 10 and 24 in cleaning, the seeds being larger.

Thyme.—This must be sown during the latter part of April, in the same manner as directed for Celery seed, and transplanted and otherwise treated as directed for Sweet Marjoram. This, like Sage, will survive the winter, and may be divided and reset in the spring, which is also the best plan in growing the seed, and as the plants will grow strong the distance should be fifteen inches each way. Cut when in blossom. The seed is produced in the same manner as Sage, and, like Marjoram, is extremely small. It ripens more unevenly than any other with which we have to do.

To save it, when the first commences to ripen, which may be known by its dark color and the pods becoming yellow and some dry, place sheets of heavy paper under each plant, well up to the stems; at noon and evening shake the plants well, causing the ripe seed to fall on the paper, which must be removed at night and replaced in the morning.

Of course this can not be done during rainy weather, but there is little danger of the seed shelling out when the air is damp. When the bulk of the seed has been thus collected, the stems may be cut, dried, thrashed, or rubbed, and the seed cleaned, all as directed for Sweet Marjoram.

The variety known as "Spreading Thyme" is the only one fit for cultivation. Herb seeds are not considered good more than two years.

HORSERADISH.

This is a very important and profitable crop with market-gardeners, and is particularly adapted to shipping, hence may be grown remote from market where the soil is suited to its cultivation. It is propagated from sets, as it does not produce seed; hence there are no varieties. In its native state it is usually found in low places, being fond of moisture. This latter fact formerly induced gardeners to plant it in low ground, which always gave it a luxuriant growth of leaves, but the root, which is the only eatable part, produced laterals and fibers, and the proportion of marketable roots was comparatively small. When planted on higher ground it was found that the roots, in searching for their favorite moisture, grew perpendicularly, and with only sufficient laterals for sets, for future planting, thus concentrating into marketable substance much that in the first instance was worthless, and only a drain upon the soil.

Soil and Preparation.—The soil best adapted to this crop is a deep loam, with mellow or free subsoil, and succeeds best on land which has been well worked and manured for a number of years. If grown separately, forty two-horse loads of stable-manure plowed in, or one ton of bone-dust, or one half a ton of guano harrowed in, should be applied to the acre. Plow deep, following with the lifting subsoil plow, harrow thoroughly, smooth the surface with the back of the harrow, and mark out rows thirty inches apart.

Gardeners grow this as a second crop, usually between the rows of early cabbages, and in this case the perfect preparation of the soil for that crop answers for this.

The land is marked with a fifteen-inch marker, every other row planted with cabbages or other crop, as the case may be, and the horseradish set in the intervening rows.

Planting and Cultivation.—The sets may be planted early in spring, but when in connection with another crop usually about the first of May, to give the first crop a chance to mature before the second requires the whole ground. Along the rows make holes, eighteen inches apart, and three or four inches deeper than the length of the sets, using a light crowbar for the purpose. In these holes drop the sets, the tops of which should be three or four inches below the surface, and fill the hole with earth, pressed to the roots by means of a dibble. The object of this deep planting is to retard the growth when cultivated as a second crop, and to give the first crop a chance to mature, for if allowed an early start the rapid growth of the large and numerous leaves would soon envelop the other crop to its destruction. With the best of care the horseradish may come on too rapidly, in which case the leaves that appear above ground may be cut off with a hoe, without materially injuring the roots. When grown alone, this deep planting is not imperative, but is advisable, for then, just as the leaves begin to appear, the whole land may be harrowed over, as is frequently practised by farmers with potatoes, thus quickly destroying the first crop of weeds. The after-cultivation is only to keep the land free from weeds, and as the leaves soon shade the ground, one thorough cultivating and hoeing is all that will be required. The sets for a start may be obtained from market-gardeners or seed-stores, and directions for preparing them for future supply will be given more particularly hereafter.

Gathering and Storing.—Horseradish should always be sold after one year's growth. The principal demand for this vegetable is in the winter, hence the roots are taken up in the fall, usually after all other crops are secured, and placed in pits as directed in the chapter on storing roots, or they may be put in a cool cellar and covered with sand.

The main root, which is the most important, penetrates deep, and requires considerable labor to secure it whole.

A deep furrow may be plowed away from the row to assist the operation, but the main labor must be done by the spade. It is desirable to remove the roots as nearly whole as possible, for the small pieces are apt to vegetate the following year, and cause some annoyance if the land is cropped with small stuff. They can be worked out by planting such crops the following year as require repeated workings with the cultivator and hoe.

Preparing for Market.—During the winter the roots, as wanted, may be removed to the market-house, the crowns nicely trimmed, all lateral roots removed except the larger ones, which may be shortened and remain attached to the main root, for sale.

They must next be cleanly washed, and laid in barrels in which holes have been bored to let the water pass away, or they may be drained and packed in boxes for shipping.

The roots are always sold by weight. In the process of preparing for market, the "sets" are saved. These are simply the lateral roots, which are cut from the main root, usually three eighths of an inch or more in diameter, and are cut about six inches long, the upper end squared off, and the bottom or root end made slanting, to serve as a guide in setting, to prevent planting upside down.

These sets should be placed in boxes, with an abundance of sand under, over, and among them, to prevent heating, the boxes placed in a cool cellar or in the pits from which the large roots were taken, protected from severe frost, and there remain until wanted for planting.

At the distance herein given nearly twelve thousand sets are required for an acre.

KALE.

This is but comparatively little grown in this country, excepting the variety called "Siberian" or "Dwarf German Greens," and more commonly known as "Sprouts" in and about New York City. For the latter market it is very extensively grown, and immense quantities of it are sold there annually.

This variety in its prime would seem like a cross between the Russia turnip and the Savoy cabbage, in form like the tops of the former, but lacking the bulbous root, and with its deep curled foliage resembling the latter, minus the solid head.

It succeeds best in a rather light soil, which must be highly manured; at least thirty two-horse loads, or bone-dust at the rate of one ton to the acre. The former must be plowed in, or the latter harrowed in. The seed should be sown about the fifteenth of August.

The ground being thoroughly prepared, mark out rows, eighteen inches apart; sow the seed evenly, and cover by raking lengthwise.

When the plants are fairly up, use the push-hoe, and thin to six inches apart. They will not require any further attention, though if the time can be spared, a dressing with the hoe may assist them to grow strong, and the better to withstand the winter.

As early as possible in the spring loosen the ground thoroughly by means of a prong-hoe, which is all the cultivation necessary. They are marketable by the first of May, and are cut in a bunch, the dead leaves trimmed away, and sold by the barrel.

They are sometimes sold very late, even when the top is in bloom, this part being cut away. Those who are growing choice cabbage seed must not have this kale in bloom anywhere near them, as it mixes very readily with the former. To grow the seed of this the same treatment is necessary as when grown for market. In spring remove all that have single leaves, as its beauty consists in the curled leaf. When the seed is ripe, which may be known by the bulk of it becoming dry, it must be cut, choosing a damp time, or early in the morning while the dew is on, and even then very careful handling is necessary to prevent shelling.

After a day or two the whole will be fit to thrash, which can be very easily done, and the seed separated from the chaff by the fan-mill, and after having been spread out in a loft for ten days, may be finally cleaned by the fan-mill and No. 20 sieve. The seed retains its vitality four years.

LEEK.

Extensively grown by market-gardeners as a second crop. From the fact that it must be washed and bunched for market, it is not a desirable crop to grow for shipping, as in this state it soon heats when packed, and quickly decays. Gardeners prefer American-grown seed, and hence I notice it here more particularly, as being of interest to the seed-grower.

Sowing Seed and Growing the Plants.—Early in spring select a piece of rich ground; plow, harrow, and rake fine; mark rows with the ten-inch marker, one and a half inch deep; sow the seeds moderately thin, and cover by raking in. One ounce of seed will produce four thousand plants. When well up, work between the rows with a push hoe; remove all weeds in the rows by hand; afterward give a deep hoeing and keep free from weeds.

Soil and Preparation.—The leek requires a strong, very rich soil, and is generally grown after a crop which has been very highly manured. The early crop being removed, clean off all weeds and rubbish, plow deep, harrow fine, and smooth with the back of the harrow, mark rows with the fifteen-inch marker, and be prepared for a wet day for transplanting. This plant is not so sensitive to drouth as some others, and may be set when the earth is only moderately wet, when celery, for instance, could not be set out with safety.

Planting and Cultivation.—The season of planting is the latter part of July. The plants may be set six inches apart in the rows already marked out, requiring about seventy thousand for an acre.

The plants should be raised by a spade, carefully drawn out, held evenly in one hand, and the loose roots and leaves cut back one half. Plant deep, pressing the earth firm to the root with the dibble. Push-hoe after planting, and later give a deep hoeing, pulling all weeds from the rows by hand; repeat the push-hoeing and weeding occasionally.

Preparing for Market.—Dig the plants, peel off the decayed leaves, cut back the roots and tops, wash, and tie in round bunches of six to eight. Leeks may be stored for winter the same as celery.

Seed.—They are grown for seed the same as for market, but should be in beds of six rows only, to facilitate cutting. They stand the winter without protection, and in spring will require deep hoeing, and to be kept clean so long as they can be worked. The after-treatment is in all respects precisely the same as for onion seed, which is given in detail under that head. The final cleaning must be given by No. 18 sieve, as the seed is smaller than that of the onion.

Leek seed can not be depended on more than one year, but if well kept a fair proportion will germinate the second season.

Varieties.—The varieties are not numerous, the most popular being known among gardeners as the

Large Flag.—The main point of this is its broad flat leaves, whence its name.

LETTUCE

This is a very important crop with market-gardeners, and large quantities are annually grown in the open air, and much is grown during winter in hot-beds, and extensively in cold-frames, some using over one thousand sashes for this purpose.

It is quite perishable, especially when it has been forced, hence it can not be recommended as a very desirable article to send long distances to market. It is, however, of importance to the seed-grower, as large quantities of seed are annually used, and all gardeners prefer the American-grown seed.

Sowing Seed and Growing Plants.—Directions are given for sowing the seed in the fall, and wintering the plants, in the chapter on cold-frames. This is decidedly the best plan when they are intended for seed, as by it each plant, when transplanted, grows large, forms a head, the stock can be kept pure, and the seed is produced more abundantly early in the season, and of better quality than when grown late.

To grow plants in a hot-bed, prepare as directed under that head, about the middle of March; level the surface, put on an inch of sifted soil, spread the seed *thin*, cover one half an inch with fine soil, and water lightly. When the plants are up, give plenty of air; keep the earth moist but not wet, and before planting harden them off, by removing the sashes a few days in advance. Good plants may be grown, not quite so early, in a cold-frame, preparing and sowing the same as in the hot-bed, but as there is no bottom heat, the sashes must be kept closer. It is very important to sow *thin*, to produce good stocky plants. An ounce to four sashes properly sown will give five to seven thousand plants. When it is desirable to have a succession of heads for marketing, the seed may be sown at intervals, in the same manner as in the fall for wintering, as directed in the chapter on cold-frames.

Soil and Preparation.—When grown for market, lettuce should have rich soil, but when grown for seed one half the usual amount of manure will suffice, for I find that in very rich land the stalks decay at the root when in blossom, and much loss is occasioned by blight. The soil should be a moderately light loam.

To grow for marketing, apply forty two-horse loads of stable-manure plowed in, or two thousand pounds of bone-flour, or one thousand pounds of guano, harrowed in, to the acre. For seed purposes, one half or less. Plow deep, harrow fine, and smooth with the back of the harrow. Mark rows with the fifteen-inch marker.

Planting and Cultivation.—Set the plants out as early as possible after the ground is dry enough to work well, and always right after the ground is prepared, while the surface is still moist. Plant them fifteen inches apart in the row, pressing the earth firmly about the root, but avoid very deep planting, as lettuce, to do well, must be entirely above ground. It may be grown between the rows of early cabbages, etc., and will come off in time to allow the ground to be cultivated and worked for the benefit of the other crop. About twenty-eight thousand plants will be required for an acre, at fifteen inches each way, or nearly forty-four thousand at one foot each way, at which distance the small varieties may be grown for market, but for seed-growing they require room to branch out, and the distance first named is preferable. Work with a push-hoe both ways; later, hoe thoroughly and deeply, removing weeds from about the plants by hand. An additional push-hoeing will usually suffice to carry the crop through clean, except in seed-growing, when it may be necessary to go through with a *narrow* push-hoe, when the plants are nearly in bloom. Hardy lettuce may be sown thinly in rows fifteen inches apart about the middle of September, and by lightly covering with coarse litter or straw will survive the winter, and may be cut in spring and sold by measure, or thinned and allowed to head. The tender varieties may also be sown in the same manner early in spring, and be marketed in the same way.

Forcing.—To grow lettuce in winter, make a hot-bed with five or six inches of soil, and when tempered, set out the plants, about eight inches apart each way.

This should be made in a very warm, sheltered position, and great care is required to guard against sudden changes. Air may be given very fine days, but as lettuce under glass is hardly expected to *head*, it may be forced rapidly, and a well-made hot-bed will bear a second crop. Gardeners about New York grow lettuce extensively in cold-frames. In addition to the frame in which the plants are preserved, they have spare frames which are covered with coarse manure or litter in the fall, and during February and March this is removed, the earth spaded up, and the plants set about eight inches each way, covered by sashes, and afterwards treated as coldframes, except as the object is to force the plants they are kept quite close, and allowed more moisture.

Marketing.—When the plants have formed heads (which, by the way, never get solid as that term is applied to cabbage), they are fit to cut. This applies to open-air culture, those growing under glass seldom forming much head. Cut them close to the ground; remove to the market-house; trim off the outer or decayed leaves; rinse in clean water, and pack lightly in well-ventilated barrels.

Seed.—When the stock is pure, there is little choice to be made. It is best to go over the bed when the heads are in their prime, and remove all such as will not head or that show signs of impurity, if any there be. For stock seed, select such as are extra fine, and by the side of each head firmly set a tall stick as a mark, when the seed from all such plants may be saved by itself. When the seed is ripe, the heads in which it is contained become plump and yellow, but as it ripens very unevenly, the only way is to average the whole. For instance, some stalks will show more than one half of the heads to be ripe, when the stalk must be cut off, although there may be blossoms still on the same plant; but if left for these blossoms to set and ripen, the first and best seed will fall out and be lost. The stalks will require two or three cuttings, as some will be more advanced than others. The small branches to which the seed-heads are attached must be cut from the stalks upon cloths, exposed to the sun until dry, and thrashed. The cleaning of lettuce-seed is often quite tedious, especially if there be much wet weather when the blossoms are shedding, for then they are apt to curl up and adhere to the seed-head, forming a ball of about the same size and weight as the seed, which renders the separation quite troublesome.

When the seed is thrashed, remove the stems by raking off. There will always be some heads not thrashed; these must be separated from the seed by No. 5 sieve, put into a bag, and again thrashed.

The whole may be sifted with Nos. 8, 10, and 14 sieves in succession, each time gathering the chaff from the top, and casting away the litter remaining in the sieve. The work may be assisted by sifting on cloths in the open air, with a gentle breeze stirring to carry away the small chaff; or where large quantities are grown, the fan-mill may be brought in use, but the sieves will in all cases be required to perfect the cleaning.

Give the final touch with sieve No. 24, which will remove the heavy dust or sand, and put away in bags.

Lettuce-seed will germinate when three years old.

Varieties.—The varieties are numerous, though but few kinds are in general cultivation in this country, and these are quite distinct.

Early Curled Silesia.—This was formerly the leading variety, and the seed is still extensively sold in seed-stores, but with market-gardeners superseded by the "Simpson," which it resembles, though smaller and not as certain to head.

Simpson's Silesia.—An improvement on the "Silesia," originated some years ago by a market-gardener then at Brooklyn, N. Y., whose name the variety still bears. Heads large and full; leaves spreading, clear greenish yellow, curled, crisp, and tender. The main variety for forcing, and the general favorite about New York.

White-seeded Butter.—Heads small, compact, and solid; lively rich yellow; leaves smooth and close; excellent flavor, unsurpassed for summer culture.

Black-seeded Butter.—Heads medium, prominent, and solid; rich yellow; flavor excellent; leaves spreading, dark green; valuable for second early.

Curled India.—Heads large and prominent, compact out not very solid; leaves curled, spreading; color, greenish yellow, with a distinct brown tinge. The best *curled* variety for summer culture.

Hardy Green or Winter.—This is the most hardy of all the varieties, and is frequently sown in September, in rows covered lightly with straw, and in the spring marketed as "cut" lettuce, and sold by measure. Heads medium size and compact, tough; leaves flat and spreading, dull green, brown-tinged; heads up very quick in spring, and used to some extent to plant among early cabbages, but is not salable when the "Simpson" comes in abundance.

MELON—Musk.

Melons are not grown in market-gardens, but for farm-gardens are an important crop, as they may be shipped any reasonable distance, and usually command paying prices, especially when grown early.

Soil and Preparation.—The soil best adapted to muskmelons is a light loam, and they do well in such as is largely composed of sand. Old sward land is preferable to fallow ground.

The land should be plowed, well harrowed, and furrowed out six feet one way by three feet the other.

At the intersections, put a shovelful of well-rotted manure or compost, and thoroughly mix it with the soil, drawing a little fine soil over the whole, making the hill broad and flat, slightly concave in the center, to receive the seed. The season of planting is from the first to the twentieth of May, and to avoid a useless repetition, I would say that the planting and after-cultivation is the same as directed for cucumbers. They are liable to be attacked by the same "striped-bug," against which I advise the same precaution and remedy. In fact, the general remarks in regard to the cucumber are applicable to this plant.

Gathering for Market.—Muskmelons are marketable only before they turn yellow, and are ripe when the stem cracks away from the fruit, at which time they should be gathered and carefully placed in barrels for shipping. They must be gathered every day during their season, for they soon become yellow and soft after they are ripe.

Seed.—When intended for seed, melons need not be gathered until quite yellow.

They should be cut open, the seeds scraped out and treated the same as cucumber-seed. The fruit after the seed is removed serves as an excellent food for cattle and hogs.

Stock seed should be saved from the earliest and best flavored of those which are used for home consumption. The seed is good for ten years.

Varieties.—The distinct varieties are not numerous, though there are many sub-varieties of almost every sort.

Citron.—Fruit of medium size, nearly round, flattened at the ends; skin green and much netted; flesh thick and fine flavored.

Nutmeg.—Fruit oval, whence the name; otherwise, very similar to the above.

Skillman's Fine-netted.—Fruit round, medium size; skin green and very closely netted, whence the name; flesh thick, fine-grained, and excellent; one of the very best varieties.

Allen's Superb.—A sub-variety of the citron. Fruit very large; skin green and much netted; flesh thick, green, solid, and excellent.

Early Christiana.—Fruit medium size; skin dark green, seldom netted; flesh deep yellow, thick, fine-grained, and excellent. Valuable for private gardens, but on account of the color not very salable.

White Japan.—Fruit small to medium; skin smooth, white, and seldom netted; flesh white, and of fair quality.

Long Persian.—Fruit large, often ten to twelve inches in length; skin green, somewhat netted; flesh thick, green, and well-flavored.

MELON—WATER.

Like the preceding, this is an important crop for the farm-garden where the soil is suitable, and large quantities are annually brought from the Southern States to our Northern markets by vessel, which, by the way, is a very convenient way of shipping where such means are at command. They are also extensively grown in New Jersey, and in other sections North where the soil is adapted to them.

Soil and Preparation.—The soil should be light, more sandy than otherwise, and new ground or old sward-land is far the best.

The season of planting is the same as for muskmelons, and the preparation the same, except the hills should be twice as far apart, that is, six by twelve feet, and one half more manure may be added to advantage.

The remarks in the preceding article on muskmelons, in regard to cultivation, may be applied to these.

Gathering for Market.—Watermelons should be marketed when *ripe*, for if allowed to become *over-ripe* the flesh will become mealy and nearly tasteless. The question may here arise: "When is a watermelon ripe?" Some judge by the curl at the stem, which becomes dry when the fruit is ripe, but it sometimes happens that the curl, and even a part or the whole of the vine, dies, and the melon is still green, hence this is not a sure test. Others press the melon with the hand, and if ripe the flesh within cracks, which may be known by the sound emitted; but this is injurious to the fruit, and hence objectionable. The surest and safest test is by sight, feeling, and sounding, which, however, requires some practice and experience to enable one to judge unmistakably. When ripe, the color of the skin is duller than when growing, the rind or outer flesh is spongy when growing, but firm when mature, and there is a peculiar sound created within the ripe fruit when smartly "snapped" by the middle finger which can not be described, but with which the ear soon becomes familiar by practice.

Therefore, the only way to acquire facility in this is to notice the color, compare the feeling and sound between known unripe and supposed ripe fruit, and determine by cutting the latter. But very few trials will give the requisite knowledge, and these may be made on the first melons before enough are ripe to make it an object to market them, and what few may be spoiled will be more than paid for in the knowledge gained, which once acquired can never be forgotten.

Seed.—Those intended for seed can be left until "dead-ripe," and when removed to the barn they will make a good job for a rainy day, when the seeds can be scraped out, placed in barrels, and after fermenting three days be washed out, using No. 2 sieve, and otherwise treated as directed for cucumber-seed.

Attention should be paid to selecting the best and finest flavored specimens for stock seed. The seed retains its vitality ten years.

Varieties.—The varieties are quite numerous, and many are quite distinct. They easily mix in the blossom, hence the necessity of growing different varieties at long distances from each other, and to avoid growing them near cucumbers, pumpkins, or the like, with which they may become mixed and spoiled.

Mountain Sweet.—This has long been a very popular and leading market variety. Fruit large, long, and slender, narrower near the stem than elsewhere; skin rather dark, sometimes marbled with various shades of green; flesh bright red, solid, and well-flavored; seeds dark brown and drab-mottled.

Mountain Sprout.—Another very popular variety. In size, shape, and flesh, similar to the Mountain Sweet; skin striped and marbled with light and darker green; seeds dun-colored.

Black Spanish.—Once very popular, but now rarely to be found pure. Fruit large, and nearly round, somewhat ribbed; skin very dark green; flesh bright scarlet, crisp, and fine flavored; seeds nearly black, tinged with brown at the small end.

Gipsy.—A comparatively new variety. Fruit medium size, oval, and evenly formed; skin beautifully marbled with pale green and dull white; flesh rosy red, crisp, and most excellently flavored; seeds small, pale, dun-colored, distinctly marked with brown at the small end.

Citron.—This variety is grown and sold to some extent for preserving. Fruit small, round, and even; skin light and dark green, striped and marbled; flesh pinkish white, solid, and without flavor; seeds red.

OKRA.

Okra or Gombo is most generally grown at the South. I well remember, when my father was engaged in market-gardening he always planted a few rows of okra, and the product was readily sold in New York at remunerative prices, and there is no doubt a limited quantity may be annually grown in the farm-garden with profit.

Cultivation.—It requires plenty of manure and light soil, and may be cultivated in the same manner as sweet corn. The seeds should not be planted before the middle of May. It is well to use plenty of seed, as some are liable to rot, and when the plants are nicely up thin to four in a hill, or twelve inches apart when grown in rows.

Cutting for Market.—The pods are edible when about half-grown, or before the upper part has become hard, when they should be cut and shipped in open barrels.

Seed.—The pods are ribbed, and contain an abundance of seeds, which lay in rows under each rib. When ripe, which may be known by the pods cracking open, they should be cut and put in a loft to dry, when they may be thrashed in bags, or opened by hand, giving the pod a sudden twist, and shelling the seeds into a sieve. I much prefer this plan, as the seeds are not so apt to be broken, and the work may be done of evenings, rainy days, or at odd spells.

It can be easily cleaned by the fan-mill or a good breeze and a No. 8 sieve. The seed is not good more than two years.

Varieties.—The varieties usually grown are the "tall" and "dwarf," the former growing six feet high, and producing long slender pods; the latter three feet high, with short thick pods, and is considered more productive than the former, which however produces the most showy pods for market.

ONION.

This is a very important crop, both to the market-gardener and for the farm-garden. Its culture is simple, the demand large, and the crop most generally a paying one. Perhaps I can not express myself more comprehensively on this subject than to give entire an article entitled "Onion

Culture" which I wrote for the "Greenpoint (L. I:) Times," with some additional remarks.

"The high price obtained for this vegetable for several years past has attracted the attention of farmers in those sections where the soil and climate are adapted to its cultivation. South of New York, as a rule, onions can not be grown to any degree of perfection, direct from the seed, not even in the market-gardens of New Jersey, and the vicinity of New York City, and those adjacent to Philadelphia, all of which, perhaps, contain the finest gardening soil in the United States.

"Gardeners in the sections named, find it necessary to use what are termed 'sets,' which are produced by sowing the seed very thick, in rather poor soil, and in midsummer; when the tops become dry, they are taken up with trowel and sieve, placed thinly in lofts to dry, and upon the approach of very cold weather put in heaps and covered with straw mats, straw, or hay.

"During the fall they are overhauled, and all that are much larger than a marble are taken out and sold for 'pickling onions,' or sometimes are planted about the first of September, becoming quite strong by winter, and are sold early in spring as green onions. These larger sets, or 'rareripes,' as they are usually called, would run to seed in time, so they must be disposed of before the seed-stalks form. The small sets are planted as early in spring as the ground can be worked. The land is kept rich by being every year *very highly* manured. It is plowed deep, finely harrowed, and smoothed, and rows marked out with a drill containing seven to ten teeth, set ten inches apart. The sets are placed about two inches apart in the rows, pressed in with the thumb and finger, and raked over with a wooden rake. Six rows constitute a bed, every seventh drill being left for a path, from which three rows on either side can be weeded at a time. The onions from these sets are sold mostly in bunches while green, to clear the ground for a second crop, some being left to dry, for as they mature much earlier than those in sections where they are produced direct from seed, usually command high prices.

"Onion sets form an important article in the stock of seedsmen, as they send thousands of bushels to the Southern States annually.

"The soil and climate of the eastern part of Long Island, and those portions of the New England States bordering on the Sound and salt-water bays, seem to be especially adapted to the production of onions from seed, and there is perhaps no better fertilizer for this crop than sea-weed, so abundant in these waters, worked over in the hog-pen, and composted with stable-manure, muck, fish, etc. A top-dressing of guano, ashes, or bone-flour will be beneficial in forwarding the crop, unless the land is very rich. To grow onions from seed, select a piece of light loamy land, no larger than can positively have perfect attention, and let it be such as is naturally free from weeds, and if well manured the previous year so much the better.

"If it has not been fall-plowed, let it be cleared of all vines, grass, or rubbish; plow in narrow furrows eight inches deep, harrow thoroughly, and smooth with the back of the harrow, then apply the manure, forty two-horse loads to the acre, which should be partly decomposed; spread it evenly, and plow again.

"In replowing have the manure scraped into the furrows, that it may be all covered; apply guano, bone, or ashes if to be used, again harrow well, and smooth the surface. Stretch a line straight on either side, and mark the rows with a drill made in the shape of a T, with wooden teeth nailed on the cross-piece, any required distance apart, lapping the outer tooth in the inner drill, and so on until the bed is finished.

"I adopt the plan described above, that is, ten-inch

rows, leaving every seventh drill for a path, but some prefer twelve and others fourteen and sixteen inches space between the rows, sowing every drill. Use a seed-sower for depositing the seed, as it can be done easier, quicker, and more evenly than by hand, and cover with a common wooden rake. From three to five pounds of seed will be required for an acre, and until the ground has become rich sow very thin.

"The same land may be used for an indefinite time. Be sure to use only new seed, as it is not sure to grow the second year, and is entirely worthless thereafter. As soon as the rows can be plainly seen, loosen the soil with a push or scuffle hoe, running close to the rows, and when necessary weed in the rows by hand, repeating as often as requisite to keep clean, but avoid cutting the onions as they begin to form. The common hoe may be used to advantage the second cleaning, to loosen the soil. Should there be places where they are in bunches, which sometimes will happen, they may be thinned to one or two inches apart. When the tops have become nearly dry pull the onion, lay in rows, and when thoroughly dry cut away the tops and store the onions in a cool, dry place, if they are to be kept, choosing a dry time for this business. Unless one has suitable storage room it is as well to sell the crop from the field, and though the price may not be so high as in winter or spring yet the risks of spoiling are avoided. The main varieties of onions are Large Red, Yellow Dutch, Yellow Danvers, and White Portugal; the first being considered the best for main crop from seed, and is the favorite in market, the second the most suitable for sets.

"In conclusion I would say to those who contemplate onion culture, try it on a small scale at first, and after ascertaining by experience the amount of labor necessary to be performed on a given quantity of land, cost of manures, etc., as well as the amount of money to be realized from a crop, it can be determined whether it will pay."

The foregoing article explains the general method of growing the crop, but as I propose to make every subject complete, I will also give directions for marketing, growing the seed, etc.

Preparing for Market. — The ripe onions may be shipped in bags or barrels, and should only be packed when thoroughly dry.

Green onions from sets are marketed in bunches when scarcely half-grown, and from thence until the tops are dry, using twelve to a bunch at first, and reducing the number to six or seven as they increase in size.

It is well to use such as show signs of running to seed, first, as they do not form large bulbs, but are quite as good as any when young.

The onions must be pulled, removed to the market-house, divested of decaying outer leaves, nicely washed, and tied in round bunches.

When the tops have become partially dry and the bulb nearly ripe, they may be bunched without washing.

Growing Sets. — Onion sets now form an important article in the seedsman's stock, and may be grown with profit by the seed-grower who has land suited to their production.

The ground should be of a light character, free from stones or gravel, in good condition, though not rich, and be prepared the same as directed for growing the onions, excepting of course the manure. Sow very early in the spring. Mark out rows ten inches apart, sowing six rows to a bed, and leaving every seventh for a path, using *thirty* pounds of seed to the acre, that they may be very thick, to prevent them growing large, the object of which has been already explained, and I may here add that the smaller the sets the better, and the higher price they will command, those scarcely larger than Marrowfat peas being preferred by gardeners to a larger size.

They must be kept scrupulously clean, and if the growth is over-rank the tops must be pressed down by rolling, or otherwise, to cause the roots to "bulb." When the tops are partially dry, cut or shear them off, lift the sets by running a trowel under them, casting into a No. 3 sieve, by which the earth can be removed. Expose them for a few days to the sun and air, covering at night. When fairly dry, store in lofts, three or four inches thick, and upon the approach of cold weather place them in heaps and cover with mats or straw.

When needed for sale or use, run them once or twice through the fan-mill. They should not be moved or handled while in a partially frozen state, nor kept long in bulk after the cold weather is past.

Seed.—Onions for seed are grown in the same manner as for market, and may be stored and wintered over as directed for sets.

They are, however, when full grown, more easily injured by hard freezing than the sets, consequently a warm place must be selected, and more protection be given, especially with the White Portugal, which is very susceptible of injury from freezing. The selections should be made in accordance with the form, color, and general distinguishing points of the variety, and a few *extra choice* specimens be planted for stock seed. The soil in which to grow onion seed should be moderately rich, but if over-abundantly manured, the blossoms are liable to blight and no seed be produced.

As soon as the ground can be worked in the spring, plow and harrow thoroughly, turning under a light dressing of manure, unless it was well manured the previous season. Plow furrows six inches deep and three feet apart, in which set the onions four to six inches apart, and cover with a hoe. Onions for seed may be planted in the summer to good advantage, in the manner here given, provided they can be put out early, before the first of September, to insure a strong growth before winter.

They will stand the winter without protection, the seed will be produced earlier than by spring planting, and the time can be better spared than at the latter season. When the seed is ripe, which may be known by the upper part of the stalks together with the seed-pods becoming yellow, and a portion of the latter bursting open, the heads must be cut, placed in barrels, carried to the loft, and spread thin. When thoroughly dry, they may be thrashed and passed through the fan-mill.

By repeating this several times the most of the seed will be clean, but there will still remain a part mixed with such pods as have become hard, which can only be separated by washing. This is done by placing a quantity into a tub of water, stirring a few moments, and gently pouring the water off. This will remove all pods and light seed, and the heavy seed which remains in the bottom must be spread on boards to dry. The whole crop may be washed in this manner, after twice running through the fan-mill, if deemed advisable, as it will not be injured by the process, provided a clear bright day is selected for the purpose, and the seed for some time after spread thin in a loft. It must not be put in bulk until *thoroughly* dry.

The final cleaning may be accomplished by No. 14 sieve. The seed can not be depended on to germinate after one year, though a part will grow at two years old when well kept.

VARIETIES.

Large Red Wethersfield.—This is the variety principally grown from seed. Bulb round and broad, flattened at the top; skin deep red.

Yellow Danvers.—The best of the "yellows" for growing from seed. Bulb nearly round; skin brownish yellow.

Yellow Dutch.—The variety generally used for producing sets. Bulb round, broad, and flat; skin clear bright yellow.

White Portugal. — The leading "white" variety. Usually commands a good price in the market, but owing to its liability to mildew, is an uncertain crop. Does not keep well, and when grown for seed should be set out in the summer if any way possible. Bulb round, broad, and flat; skin silvery white, sometimes tinged with pink.

Potato Onion.—This does not produce seed, but is propagated by a natural increase of from four to six bulbs, which form from the parent-root. They are the earliest *dry* onions which come to market.

Plant early in spring, in light, rich soil, marking rows fifteen inches apart, three inches deep, setting the bulbs six inches apart, and entirely under ground. Around these the young bulbs form and grow, and they should be lightly covered with soil, in process of hoeing. Keep free from weeds, and when ripe treat the same as those grown from seed. They do not keep well unless carefully preserved.

PARSLEY.

The demand for this vegetable is rather limited, and as yet hardly a suitable crop for the farm-garden, but as the American seed is generally preferred, it is here noticed as being of some importance to the seed-grower. It must be sown quite early in spring, in good soil, in the same way as carrots, and afterward treated the same as that crop.

When thinned, the plants, drawn out, are bunched and sold, and later the leaves are cut from the growing plant and similarly disposed of, a bunch consisting of about as much as can be encircled by the thumb and forefinger. It can be taken up and preserved for winter use, or to transplant for seed in trenches, similar to celery, or bedded in the manner of preserving "late cabbages" for seed, partially burying the leaves, and covering lightly with coarse manure or litter. When thus kept, it is taken out, washed, and tied in bunches of three or four, the root and leaves entire. It can be sown in cold-frames, in rows twelve inches apart, and being protected by sashes, will be fit to cut in winter, at which season it formerly paid enormous profits, but now the supply exceeds the demand.

Seed.—The simplest plan is, when sowing a bed of carrots or beets, to sow every third row with parsley, thinning to six inches apart, which will give it forty-five inches between rows when the other crop is removed. When thus sown, in the fall go over and cut out all imperfect plants, ridge the earth to but not over them, and at the approach of severe cold weather cover lightly with coarse litter, which must be removed early in the spring. When taken up in the fall, as previously noticed, the roots may be set out in four-foot rows one foot apart, and in either case keep clean by cultivator and hoe.

The seed much resembles that of celery, grows and ripens the same, and the directions given for harvesting and cleaning that are applicable to this crop, using No. 20 sieve for the final cleaning. The seed will germinate when two years old.

Varieties. — The "Double Curled" and "Triple Curled" are the varieties principally grown, the "Plain" or single leaf not being salable. The former is the most hardy, and generally grown for out-door crop, the second being used for growing under glass.

PARSNIP.

This is extensively grown by market-gardeners, and is one of the leading root-crops for the farm-garden, not only with a view to growing for market, on account of its availability for shipping, but it possesses valuable properties which recommend it as a food for stock. It generally commands fair prices, and from the fact of its being comparatively non-perishable, the market is seldom glutted, and should this perchance occur, and continue through the season, the roots may be used to advantage for feeding animals.

Soil and Preparation.—Parsnips require good, strong, free soil, which may be prepared in the manner directed for carrots, using one half more manure, and as the seed is very light, and naturally weak in the germ, *thick* growing is essential. They may be sown from early spring until June, but early sowing is advisable, as the seed will not germinate well in hot, dry weather. The after-culture is exactly the same as directed for carrots, and in fact the remarks under that head in reference to harvesting, marketing, etc., are in the main applicable to this crop. Parsnips are usually taken up and stored late in the fall to be ready for winter marketing, but they are perfectly hardy, and when grown solely for seed may be left until spring, when they should be taken up, selections made, and the best transplanted, and cultivated as directed for carrots, having the rows four feet apart. The seed should never be grown in sections where the Wild Parsnip grows, as it will mix and be spoiled. The seeds are produced in clusters or heads, and two seeds always grow together, lying the one flat against the other. When these seeds part, the heads should be cut, as such are ripe, and after drying in a loft, they can be thrashed, passed through the fan-mill twice, and cleaned by No. 10 sieve.

It ripens unevenly and requires repeated cuttings. It will seldom germinate more than one year.

Varieties.—That known as the "Long Smooth Cup"

or "Hollow-Crowned" is the only variety grown to any extent for marketing.

PEA.

This is extensively cultivated for market, generally in the farm-gardens not very remote from the place of sale, except so far as its cultivation in the Southern States is concerned. There quantities are raised for New York and other Northern markets, and in consequence prices for "home-grown" peas are not so good as they might be, were it not for this competition.

Still, when Northern peas come to market the others soon disappear, as those fresh-picked are far superior in flavor to such as have been shipped. Early peas, for Northern growers, may not be considered a *very* profitable crop in general, but they come in when there is but little else for market, and, as an old Dutch gardener once remarked, they bring in some "early monish," and beside the ground is cleared in time and left in good condition for a second crop.

Marrowfat peas, from their more prolific yield and higher prices obtained, bring better returns, but the land can not be cleared so early.

Soil and Preparation.—Peas require a light soil, and to get an abundant yield, a liberal quantity of manure must be applied.

Land lying to the southward and sheltered from the north winds is preferable for early peas, as it is important to have them in market as early as possible to obtain the best prices. Plow and harrow well; mark out furrows six inches deep, four feet apart for the early, and five feet for the late varieties.

Spread well-rotted manure or compost in the furrows, allowing a good shovelful to one yard of row.

Sowing and Cultivation.—Early peas must be sown as

soon as the ground can be worked, and may be the first crop planted. Sow quite thick in the rows on the manure, covering with a rake or hoe to a depth of three inches or more. When deep planted, they will produce the most. As soon as they are up, use the cultivator and hoe, which repeat twice, pulling weeds from the rows by hand. When grown on a large scale, it will not pay to "brush" the vines, and if allowed to lay long in one position, the part of the vine below will rot; therefore, every day or two after the vines have fallen down they must be laid over by means of a hoe-handle, turning one way one day, and reversing the next. This must be done until the peas are fit for market, and when grown for seed, continued occasionally until they are ripe.

Marketing.—When the pods have filled out plump, and before they become hard, they are marketable, and must be plucked, being careful not to tear the vines out in handling, and may be put in bags or open barrels for shipping, except when sent long distances, in which case small crates are preferable, as peas are very liable to heat and decay when long packed in heavy bulk. The picking is often done in a great measure by German women, and where such help can be obtained, it is the best for this and similar purposes.

Seed.—The bulk of peas sold in this country for seed are grown in Europe, principally in England, where they are produced quite cheaply, and free from the "bug" which is so common in American-grown peas. The egg of the insect is laid in the blossom or in the young pea, where it hatches, producing an insect of considerable size known as the "pea-bug," which eats its way *out*, leaving a hole in the pea, which spoils the appearance, but does not in the least affect the vitality, as the germ is never destroyed.

Gardeners who understand this prefer American-grown

seed for early planting. The manner of growing for seed is the same as for market, as is also the after-treatment.

When the pods begin to dry, the seed is ripe, and the vines must then be pulled, and allowed to lie a day or two, but it is very important to get them thrashed as soon as dry, for if they should get wet after becoming ripe, the chances are that much of the seed will be spoiled.

They can be easily thrashed with a flail, taking care not to break the seed, and can be readily cleaned by the fan-mill.

They should be spread thin in a loft, and allowed to become perfectly dry before being packed.

The seed retains its vitality two years.

Varieties.—More or less of the choice European varieties are planted for market, but the larger growers prefer the

Philadelphia Extra Early.—This is of good size, full, plump pods, and the earliest variety grown which has the necessary requisites. Vine two and a half feet.

Marrowfat—White and Black-eyed.—There are many Marrow peas, especially the wrinkled varieties, which are far superior to these in flavor, but which do not possess the requisites for marketing, hence these old varieties are still extensively cultivated for this purpose. Pods large and plump; vine about four feet, and abundant bearers.

PEPPER.

Grown to some extent for market, and almost universally in private gardens, hence more or less seed is in demand. The seed may be sown in hot-beds the same as the egg-plant, it requiring considerable moisture to swell it; the plants are to be thinned to three inches each way, or may be transplanted at that distance into a new hot-bed. They require a loamy soil and an abundance of manure. Plant the latter part of May, in rows three feet apart, and eighteen inches between the plants.

Marketing.—The fruit is marketable when about half-grown, though some may be sold when ripe, and may be shipped in open barrels or crates. They should be cut with a part of the stem, but never broken from the plant.

Seed.—The seed is produced about the core attached to the stem within the pods, and is ripe when the pods are red and begin to shrivel, at which time the fruit may be gathered, mashed or ground, and the seed washed out the same as that of the egg-plant.

The seed retains its vitality two years.

Varieties.—The varieties are quite numerous, the leading sorts being the Bell or Bull-Nose and the Squash. They are both red when ripe, the former large, quite blunt and uneven at the lower or blossom end, but sometimes tapering. The latter is about one third as large as the Bell, in shape broad and flat, very similar to a Tea-plate squash.

POTATOES.

There is perhaps no vegetable grown in which the public are so much interested as the potato, and many farmers count upon it as one of their main crops. Of late years, however, the uncertainty of getting a crop renders it hazardous to plant largely.

To those who have seen the tremendous yields of this esculent in years gone by, there naturally arises in their minds the query: "What is the cause of the failure of the potato-crop of late years?" "Is it because the soil has become exhausted of some particular ingredient?" or "Have the seasons changed sufficiently to produce a damaging effect?" or "Is it not more likely the seed has run out by long-continued planting from the same stock, and too frequently the use of small or inferior seed?"

It is an established fact that all vegetables are improved by changing, that is, getting seed from a distance, and from soil and climate varying from that in which it is to be planted. This theory would seem to be established with regard to the potato when we consider what great results have been achieved with the new varieties recently disseminated. Take for instance the Early Rose, which in some cases has yielded more than one hundred and twenty-five and quite commonly one hundred pounds from one pound of seed. So with the Peerless, which wherever tried has proved most excellent. I might also mention a number of others which gave much better results than the old varieties under similar treatment. It is not my object to try to persuade farmers to discard the old varieties and go into new ones, though many of the latter are worth a fair trial, and every grower should test for himself. It is quite natural for a man when he wishes to save seed from garden vegetables to select the best. For instance, he saves the finest and best shaped tomatoes, the longest and smoothest cucumbers, the sweetest melons, the smoothest onions, and in fact everything having the best qualities according to its kind.

He does this because he knows they can be, and are, annually improved by this means, whereas, on the other hand, the varieties would soon run out if seed was saved promiscuously. This fact being then universally established in regard to the vegetables of the garden, is it not reasonable to attribute the failure of the potato in a great measure to the continued planting of other than choice selected seed without change ?

Soil, Preparation, and Planting.—Early potatoes, in which the farm-gardener is more particularly interested, require a loamy soil, which should be plowed moderately deep, and finely harrowed, turning under thirty two-horse loads of well-rotted manure, or harrowing in one thousand pounds of bone-flour or six hundred pounds of guano to the acre. They should be planted as early in the spring as the ground can be worked.

Mark out furrows six inches deep, thirty inches apart, in which drop the seed one foot apart, and cover with a hoe, or throw a light furrow over them with the plow, and level with the back of the harrow. Fallow ground is preferable to sward for *early* potatoes, but when sward land is to be used for this crop, the seed may be put in as the land is plowed, planting every third furrow, in the manner that farmers usually pursue, covering only three or four inches, or the land may be more deeply plowed and furrows made as above, but this can not be so readily done on sward as on fallow ground. It is far preferable, if possible, to plow the land during August of the preceding year; harrow well, and, if you please, sow flat turnips broadcast, giving at the same time a dressing of five hundred pounds of bone-flour to the acre. After the crop is taken off, plow again, and harrow thoroughly late in the fall, which will leave the land in excellent condition for the crop of the following year. Where manure is scarce, the furrows may be marked out as first mentioned, and the manure, which must be well-rotted, spread in the furrows, a good shovelful to about six feet of row, or bone-flour or guano may be applied lightly in the same manner. In regard to the various methods of planting, my observations have led me to the following conclusions. In wet seasons those manured in the row do the best, and in dry seasons those manured broadcast and *plowed in* give the best results, and in order to get between these two extremes, spread the manure broadcast, plow the ground, and furrow out, as first mentioned, which I believe to be the very best method of planting early potatoes. The seed should not be covered deeply, but may be slightly ridged, just before they come in blossom. The ground may be lightly harrowed over just as the first sprouts appear which will destroy the first crop of weeds. The after-culture is only to cultivate and hoe to keep free from weeds. Various devices have been invented for "digging" potatoes, but with the early ones at least, the spade or digging-fork is the best. Considerable loss is sustained sometimes by the ravages of the "grub," which gnaws the surface of the tubers, thus disfiguring them, and totally unfitting them for marketing.

A good dressing of shell-lime or ashes has a tendency to destroy these pests, as well as being otherwise beneficial to the crop.

Always plant perfect seed, the largest and best that can be had. Cut so as to leave two good eyes to a piece. There is much diversity of opinion on this point, as well as to what length of time a potato should be cut before planting, but I prefer the plan mentioned, and at such time as may be convenient, within a fortnight of the proposed time of planting.

Varieties.—The varieties of potatoes are numerous, and new ones are being constantly added. Many varieties have only local reputations, and even the Early Rose, so widely disseminated, and such a general favorite, fails entirely with some growers; hence, the only proper plan for a grower to determine which is the best *for himself*, is to try a few of the leading sorts.

In growing potatoes for seed, care should be taken to have every variety true to name, to use only perfect seed in planting, and to grow them in new soil if possible.

They should be perfectly ripe before digging, taken up when dry, and stored in pits or elsewhere away from frost until wanted, but avoid warm cellars, which may cause the tubers to sprout and injure them for seed.

RADISHES.

These vegetables are sold in immense quantities in all markets, and many are grown in the Southern States and shipped North. They are, however, of a very perishable nature, and soon heat when packed in bulk.

Soil, Preparation, and Sowing.—Radishes to be produced in perfection must have light, warm, and rich soil, and that which has been previously well manured is preferable to manuring at the time of sowing, as in the latter case they are apt to be attacked by a small grub, and the radishes become, to use the common phrase, "wormy," hence not marketable. If the soil requires fertilizing at the time of sowing, use bone-flour, one thousand pounds to the acre.

They may be sown broadcast, over a bed of beets or carrots just sown, and raked in with them, and will come off in time to allow the main crop to be worked. This plan is objectionable, because such crops are generally sown on fresh-manured land, hence the radishes are liable to be wormy, and then in gathering the bed must be walked over, often in wet weather, thus packing the ground, and probably damaging the main crop more than the radishes can repay. It is far preferable to plow and harrow the ground very early in the spring, sow the seed broadcast, ten pounds to the acre, and cover by raking or light harrowing. The crop will be off in time to allow of beets or carrots being sown, when the manure necessary for those crops may be applied, the ground again plowed, which will be of great benefit, the seed sown, and when ready the plants can be worked without interruption. Radishes may be sown in hotbeds alone, or a few seeds be sprinkled in at the time of sowing cabbage or lettuce seeds, or they may be sown in a cold-frame, after the plants are removed, covered with sashes, and by coming early command good prices.

The white and yellow varieties may be sown at intervals during the summer, and the Black Spanish and Chinese Rose in August, for winter use.

Marketing.—The long varieties must be tied in flat

bunches of from six to nine, and the round sorts in round bunches of similar number.

The flat bunches can more easily be washed by placing a board, sunken at one end by a weight, in a tub of water, upon which the bunch can be laid, and rubbed over with a soft brush. The round varieties can generally be cleaned by dipping a few times in water, either before or after bunching.

Pack in barrels, with holes in the bottom to allow the water to escape, or, if for a distant market, drain well and pack in small, well-ventilated crates.

Seed.—When grown for seed, sow in rows eighteen inches apart; when well up, use the push-hoe, and when of fair size thin to six inches apart, leaving such only as are true to the variety, and afterward give a deep hoeing, and remove all weeds from the rows which may have been overlooked at the time of thinning.

The Yellow Summer, Spanish, and Chinese varieties must be sown in August, wintered in pits, and set out in spring the same as turnips. Gardeners generally prefer the European seed of the scarlet varieties, as they make less tops or leaves, but the American, one year from the European seed, produces far superior radishes. The proper plan is to sow a few rows of imported seed, and from the product sow for main crop the next season; and every year, beside the main bed, put in a few rows of imported seed for stock, and so repeat. The imported will not yield much seed at first, but from that a fair crop may be had, and this will produce the finest radishes, but if continually grown from the same stock, the tops get long and the roots tough and spindling. When the seed is ripe, which may be known by the pods becoming dry, the whole may be reaped or mowed off, and left in rows, and occasionally turned until perfectly dry, when it may be thrashed. The pods are of a peculiar spongy structure, and unless perfectly dry will not break, but rather mash down by thrashing.

When thrashed, the stalks can be raked away, and the seed easily cleaned by passing twice through the fan-mill. It retains its vitality three years.

Varieties.—The varieties are numerous, but few are adopted by gardeners, the principal being the Scarlets.

Long Scarlet.—Root long, slender, growing much above ground; color deep pink, pale below ground, white at the point.

Scarlet Turnip-rooted.—Root round, otherwise similar to the above, rather deeper colored.

White Summer.—Root large, semi-long, tapering; color white, above ground greenish, and sometimes pink.

Yellow Summer.—Root large, nearly or quite round; color russet yellow.

Black Spanish.—Root large, semi-long; color dull black.

Rose Chinese Winter.—Root large, narrow at the top, growing quite thick and flat at the bottom; color deep pink above, pale pink or rose below ground.

RHUBARB.

This is extensively sold in all leading markets, and may be shipped to advantage when carefully packed.

It is propagated by parting the roots, leaving one eye to each piece of root.

The seeds rarely produce as good as the parent variety.

Soil and Planting.—It requires very rich soil, and for early, light land and a warm exposure are essential, though a heavy loam will produce the largest stalks. The land may be prepared the same as directed for asparagus, and heavy dressings of manure must be annually applied.

Mark out furrows five feet apart, and set the roots three

feet in the rows, covering the crowns about two inches. The after-cultivation consists in cultivating and hoeing, and the general manner of working is the same as directed for asparagus.

It may be grown in a forcing pit by setting large roots thick together, burying six inches with fine manure, and covering with sashes, which need seldom be opened, except to apply water, which may be applied often enough to keep the bed somewhat moist. Grown in this way it comes early and commands good prices.

Marketing.—The stalks must be pulled, trimmed, tied in bunches of three to six, and the leaves cut away one half. It may be packed in ventilated boxes for shipping.

Seed.—The seed is produced on a tall stalk thrown up from the center of the plant, and when ripe and dry may be stripped by hand.

The seed-stalks should never be allowed to grow when leaf-stalks are wanted for market. The seed retains its vitality two years.

Varieties.—The leading varieties are Linnæus for early and Victoria for main crop.

SALSIFY OR OYSTER-PLANT.

The demand for this vegetable is steadily increasing, and considerable quantities are now sold. The seed is difficult to grow, or rather to save, as small birds are very fond of it, and attack it when in the milk, while yet unfit to gather. Still, when it can be saved it is in demand, as the American seed is preferred to the imported.

Soil and Preparation.—The soil should be light and rich, and may be prepared as directed for carrots, using double the quantity of manure. The after-cultivation is the same as for that crop.

Marketing.—The roots must be trimmed, washed, and

tied in round bunches of six to eight. It is marketable in the fall, but more generally used in winter, and can be put away to use at that season in trenches like celery, or in beds like late cabbage for seed, partially covering the leaves.

Seed.—The seed is produced the second year, and the plants, being perfectly hardy, may remain in the ground for that purpose.

The seed-heads are very similar to those of the Dandelion, but much larger, and like that, when the seed is ripe, expand to a head covered with furze. The pods should be cut when about half-open, cutting the furze away at the same time.

It must be attended to several times each day in the hight, as it will soon blow away when fully expanded. It retains its vitality two years. There are no varieties.

SPINACH.

Extensively grown by market-gardeners, but not a very good article for shipping, though it may be grown to advantage in localities not very remote from market.

Soil and Preparation.—Spinach does best in a light loam, which, to grow it in perfection, must be highly manured. It may follow early cabbage, onions, or any early crop which has had a liberal manuring.

Clear the ground, plow and harrow thoroughly, and smooth the surface, turning under twenty two-horse loads of stable-manure, or harrowing in one thousand pounds of bone-flour, or five hundred pounds of guano, to the acre. Mark rows fifteen inches apart, one inch and a half deep, in which sow the seed moderately thin, using about six pounds to the acre. The season for sowing is about the tenth of September, but may be sown early in the spring, but then will not come so early into market, nor yield so heavily as when fall-sown. It is quite hardy, and may be exposed the entire winter, except in very cold localities, where a thin covering of coarse straw late in the fall will be beneficial, and which should be removed quite early in the spring. Use the push-hoe as soon as the rows can be seen, and later give a deep hoeing, which repeat again early in spring, thoroughly pulverizing the soil.

Marketing.—It will be marketable when the inner leaves have become considerably grown; then the larger plants may be cut out with a knife, and later the crop may be cut indiscriminately, by running a push-hoe under the rows, always cutting so as to have all the leaves attached to a small part of the root. The decayed ends of leaves must be cut away, after which wash and place in barrels, with holes at the bottom, and for long distances it will be advisable to drain out well before packing.

Seed.—Much spinach seed is imported, but the American-grown is considered to produce the most hardy plants, and hence is preferred by market-gardeners. It should invariably be sown in the fall to produce good seed, and otherwise grown as for market.

When the seed is ripe, which may be known by its changing from green to brown, and the leaves drying away, the stalks must be pulled, laid in rows for a day to dry, and thrashed. It ripens irregularly, and two gatherings will be necessary. After thrashing, rake away the stalks, and pass the seed twice through the fan-mill. A considerable portion will be in clusters of five or six seeds, which may be separated by rubbing through No. 5 sieve. Again pass through the fan-mill, clean with No. 14 sieve, and place in a loft on cloths to dry, before storing. The seed retains its vitality two years.

Varieties.—The varieties are few, and that known as the Round-leaved is the one in general cultivation.

SQUASHES.

These are seldom found in market-gardens; they belong properly to the farm-garden, and are well adapted for shipping. They are grown to some extent at the South for Northern markets, coming considerably earlier than we can produce them, and the season may be advanced there as well as here, by starting the early varieties on sods, in cold-frames, as directed for cucumbers, thereby also, in a measure, avoiding the "striped bug."

Soil, Planting, etc.—The soil for squashes should be a light loam.

The season for planting in the open ground is the middle of May.

The preparation is the same as for melons or cucumbers, as is also the after-cultivation. Plant the early or bush varieties five by four feet, and the late or running sorts twelve by six feet apart. The same attention must also be paid to the "striped bug," which is very destructive to these plants.

Marketing.—The early varieties are marketable when scarcely half-grown, always before the skin becomes hard, and may be shipped in barrels. They require some care in cutting and handling to avoid bruising. The late sorts must be allowed to ripen, and can be shipped in barrels or in bulk.

Seed.—Great care should be taken to grow varieties far apart, as they readily mix in the blossom, and moreover they should not be grown near melons nor anything of this nature. When ripe, which may generally be determined by the hardness of the skin, the squashes may be gathered, cut open with a hatchet, the seeds scraped out, and afterwards treated as directed for cucumber seeds.

It retains its vitality ten years.

VARIETIES.

Early Scalloped Bush.—Of this there are several sub-varieties, distinguished by their color—white, yellow, striped, etc.—of which the first two are the most popular. Plant large and compact; fruit round, scalloped about the edge, oval next the stem, flat or indented at the blossom-end.

Early Crookneck Bush.—Plant same as the above; fruit medium size, deep yellow, partly crooked, with slender neck, and covered with small wart-like bunches.

Boston Marrow.—Plant trailing; fruit medium size, egg-shaped, pointed at the ends; skin deep creamy yellow. The leading fall variety.

Hubbard.—The plant, size, and form same as the above; color dull green, brown above. The leading winter variety for market.

SWEET-POTATOES.

Universally cultivated throughout the United States, and extensively grown at the South for market. They do not stand handling so well as the common potato, being liable to rot quickly when bruised. They can be profitably grown in some parts of the Northern States where the soil is suitable, but as a general rule are not so dry and fine-flavored as when grown at the "sunny South."

Growing the Plants.—The plants may be grown in a hot-bed prepared as directed under that head, substituting sand for the common soil, or they may be started in a cold-frame in a warm position, removing the earth and using sand. They may also be grown without the aid of sashes in a common frame, in a warm and sheltered place, covering at night with boards. In a hot-bed the tubers should be started about the twentieth of April, and in a cold-frame ten days earlier. In either case put two inches of sand for the bed, cut the potatoes lengthwise, placing them thickly on the bed, cut side down, and covering with two inches of sand, which may be increased to four inches or more as the plants appear. The bed must be kept moist but not wet, and airing be attended to, especially with the hot-bed when the plants are up. As the first shoots are pulled, more will be formed and grow up. Immense quantities of plants are annually sold, and there are few localities in which a bed of plants can not be disposed of at paying prices. The potatoes for seed are usually obtained from the South, as they require a warm, dry, and even temperature to preserve them. Seed may, however, be saved at the North by digging them on a dry day, placing in a loft for a few days to dry, afterwards packing in barrels with dry sand, and storing in a dry, warm place, always handling with the greatest care, to avoid bruising.

Soil, Preparation, and Planting.—The sweet-potato requires a light soil, more sandy than otherwise, which should also be dry and warm. Plow the ground deep, harrow well, and mark out shallow furrows four feet apart. In these place well-rotted stable manure or compost, a good shovelful to a yard of row; plow the earth from both sides to and over the manure, forming a ridge; even the surface thereof, and set the plants deeply over the manure, fifteen inches apart.

The land may be marked out four feet each way, a shovelful of manure placed at the angles, and the earth raised over it, forming hills, in each of which set two good plants. In either case it is well to have the land prepared and set the plants after a rain. It is hardly safe to plant in this section before the first of June. The after-cultivation consists of hoeing the ridges and cultivating between, occasionally disturbing the vines to prevent them rooting at the joints.

Marketing.—Northern-grown sweet-potatoes do not

keep well under the best of circumstances, and hence it is advisable to commence digging early, and sell them direct from the field, finishing before frost if possible.

Varieties.—The varieties are not numerous, the "Nansemond" being the one generally conceded to be the best for a Northern climate.

TOMATOES.

They are extensively grown for market, and are an important crop for the farm-garden. Fifty years ago they were scarcely used for eating, while now hundreds of thousands of bushels are annually consumed in this country, showing that all vegetable productions create a market for themselves, a fact worthy the attention of those who from fear that the business of vegetable-growing may be overdone are deterred from planting many crops which they might grow to advantage.

Growing the Plants.—The seed may be sown in the open ground after frost, but at the North these plants will be too late to mature much of the crop, though some will ripen.

To grow them early sow the seed in March in a hot-bed, transplant into a new hot-bed, and give the same general treatment as directed for egg-plants, though they do not require quite so much heat. For seed purposes or main crop sow in hot-bed early in April, and transplant into a cold-frame, five inches each way, covering with sashes, and giving air clear days. By either of these methods, the former especially, they could be produced at the South, for the Northern market, a fortnight or more earlier than they now are.

Soil, Preparation, and Planting.— Tomatoes will grow in almost any soil, but to grow them early, that composed mostly of sand is best, and for late and abundant yield a loamy soil is preferable. The ground should be plowed, harrowed, and furrows made four feet apart for light, and five feet for heavier soils, cross-furrowing three feet apart. At the angles place a half-shovelful of well-rotted manure, which mix with the soil, leaving the mass hollow, to receive the plant. I have found bone-phosphate an excellent fertilizer for tomatoes in loamy soil, but prefer stable-manure for early crops. The planting may be done from the middle of May until the middle of June, taking up the plants with balls of earth when it can be done, and choosing a moist time for transplanting.

Marketing.—The fruit should be gathered before *fully* ripe, to be solid, and is usually marketed in baskets, holding less than a bushel, or four to a barrel. For shipping long distances small latticed crates should be used.

Seed.—Tomatoes for seed should be allowed to get perfectly ripe, when they may be gathered, ground or mashed, and placed in barrels to ferment. They may so remain for any reasonable length of time without material injury, but will be fit to wash out in forty-eight hours, and the sooner thereafter the seed is washed the brighter it will be.

Wash through Nos. 3 and 5 sieves in the manner of egg-plant. The seed is of a spongy nature and retains much moisture, and to facilitate drying, when it is taken out from the tub in No. 10 sieve, take the seed in handfuls, and press firmly to remove the water, after which spread on shutters to dry, and treat the same as all other washed seeds. The very finest fruit should be chosen for stock seed. The seed retains its vitality seven years.

Varieties.—The varieties are numerous, but comparatively few are distinct.

General Grant.—This may be considered as the earliest variety, but so far as this is concerned there is very little difference between the various sorts, under the same treatment. Fruit of medium size, flat and smooth, solid flesh, ripens very even; color deep red.

7

Large Smooth Red.—This is the leading sort about New York. Fruit large, thick, generally smooth, though sometimes irregular; solid flesh, ripens even; color bright red.

Cook's Favorite.—Fruit medium size, round, and uniformly smooth; solid flesh; ripens uneven, that is, the part next the stem is frequently quite green in color when the other part is ripe; color bright red.

Trophy.—A variety recently introduced; an improvement on the Large Smooth Red. Fruit very large, thick and heavy, very smooth, solid flesh, ripens even; color red.

TURNIPS.

These are seldom found in the market-garden, but extensively grown in farm-gardens and by regular farmers. They usually command fair prices, and when the market is glutted can be fed out to good advantage. They are a first-class article for shipping, and the Ruta-Bagas are often sent to market by boat-loads. The white, flat, early varieties are grown to a considerable extent South, and shipped to Northern markets in bunches or in bulk.

These may be grown to advantage at the North, for bunching, if sown very early. The yellow, especially the Russia or Ruta-Bagas, are the most salable in winter.

Soil and Preparation.—Turnips will grow in almost any soil which is moderately rich. An essential point is to make them grow quickly, otherwise they are apt to be tough and woody. They do best in light loamy soils, and that which has been manured for a previous crop is preferable to manuring with stable-manure at the time of sowing, as in this case they are liable to be worm-eaten and hence unsalable. Bone-flour is the best fertilizer that can be applied at the time of sowing, at the rate of six hundred pounds to the acre, broadcast, and harrowed in.

Only the past fall, I had three beds of Ruta-Bagas, one

of which was manured with stable manure, and the other two with bone-flour. The former were quite uneven and worm-eaten, while the latter were smooth and fine, and every way superior to the others. The land should be plowed and thoroughly harrowed, to reduce all lumps, and the surface smoothed by the back of the harrow.

Sowing and Cultivation.—When the flat varieties are grown early, for bunching, they had better be sown thin, in shallow drills, fifteen inches apart, push-hoed when well up, thinned to four inches apart, and afterwards have a deep hoeing.

Sow very early in the spring, using two pounds of seed to the acre.

When these or the Stone varieties are grown late for seed or winter marketing, sow the latter part of August, broadcast, one pound of seed to the acre, and harrow over lightly. The Russia or Ruta-Baga should be sown the middle of July, in drills thirty inches apart, to be worked with cultivator, or twenty inches and worked with a hoe, using one and a half to two pounds of seed to the acre. In either case they must be thinned to six or eight inches apart when fairly up, and the soil occasionally stirred.

These are liable to be attacked when young by the "cabbage or turnip flea," in which case the plants must be sprinkled with lime-dust early in the morning. One or two applications will free them from these pests.

Marketing.—Early turnips are marketable when about two inches in diameter. They can be pulled, a part of the leaves and the tap-root cut away, washed, tied in bunches of five to seven, and a part of the tops may be shorn off.

They may be shipped in well-ventilated barrels or boxes. The dry roots should be marketed in barrels or in bulk, and when kept over winter, the sprouts must be cut off, but they must not be washed.

Harvesting and Storing.—The roots should be pulled about the middle of November, topped and put away as directed in the chapter on storing for winter, always being careful not to cut away the heart of such as are intended for producing seed.

Seed.—Turnips for seed must be set out as early as the ground can be worked, to insure a full crop.

They do not require very rich ground; that which has been manured the previous season will not need any more fertilizing. When not in a fair state of fertility, apply bone-flour in the rows, a good handful to about fifteen roots, before covering. The best crop of turnip seed I ever raised was manured in this manner. The ground should be loamy and well plowed and harrowed. Mark out light furrows three feet apart, and with a dibble set the turnips fifteen inches apart, fastening the tap-root.

Cover with earth over the whole root, leaving the sprouts above ground.

They will soon start to grow, when they must be cultivated and hoed, and when they commence to blossom run the ridge-plow through and draw the earth about the roots to support them against storms. When ripe, which may be known by many of the pods becoming dry, the whole may be cut with shears or sickles. This must be done early in the morning, while the dew is still on, to prevent shelling out. When the whole is dry, carry in, thrash, and clean, as directed for cabbage seed. Avoid growing any two varieties near each other, and especially the Ruta-Baga near cabbage seed, as they readily mix.

The seed is good for four years.

Varieties.—The varieties are numerous, though but few are grown for market.

Strap Leaf Early White Dutch.—Bulb medium size; flat, white, greenish above ground; leaves narrow and few; valuable only for early use.

Strap Leaf Red Top.—Bulb medium size, flat, white, purplish red above ground. Valuable for bunching and early fall, not very salable when the Ruta-Baga is in market.

Yellow Aberdeen or Stone.—Bulb quite large, thick, nearly round, pale yellow; there are two sub-varieties, known as "Purple Top" and "Green Top" from the color above ground, the former being generally preferred.

Long White Cowhorn.—Bulb large, long, somewhat crooked, whence its name; white, tinged with green, and occasionally pink above ground; very firm in flesh and well-flavored. Very valuable for stock, and decidedly the best white turnip for family use in winter.

American Ruta-Baga or Russia Turnip.—This is the leading market variety. Bulb large, semi-long and thick, smooth, tapering at the root, bright yellow. There are two sub-varieties, distinguished like those of the Aberdeen, and the "Purple Top" is generally preferred.

General Management.—The old adage "What is worth doing at all is worth doing well" applies very forcibly to the business of growing vegetables or seeds, and it is worse than folly for any one to carry on either in a loose and careless manner, and expect to realize any profit therefrom. Supposing the soil intended for this purpose and all natural advantages to be of the best, unless fertilizers are applied to the land, commensurate with the crop taken from it, an abundant yield can not be of long duration, and it matters not how well the land has been prepared, by manuring and other means, unless the crop is taken care of after it is sown or planted, all previous labor and expense will have been in vain. To begin either branch of this business, *on a large scale*, without experience, must result in disappointment and loss, but for those among the class of men alluded to in the chapter on "Farm-Gardening," who have patience to begin in a small way, there is an inviting prospect before them. Having already noticed the importance of liberal manuring and subsequent care of the crop, I might add the great importance of *preventing*, rather than destroying, weeds; the plowing and working of the land when in proper condition; the sowing of seeds or planting at the proper time; and, in short, of doing all things in season. By early and repeated stirring of the soil, all seeds of weeds near the surface are destroyed while in the germ, and it is a grave mistake to wait until the weeds can be seen before the cultivator and hoe are resorted to. Another important point is to exercise judgment in doing the work; for instance, there is little use in hoeing or cultivating when the ground is very wet, but that is just the time to pull weeds from among the young plants in the rows; and so on, through the whole routine, endeavor to arrange the work according to the weather or season, so far as may be practicable. During the winter months preparations should be made for the spring. See that the tools and all things are in repair; cart out manure and place it in large heaps near where it is to be used, make up straw mats, mend sashes, get out strings for bunching the next season, if any are to be used, and, in short, anything that can be done should be done, to save time in the hurried season. Have enough help at hand to do the work as it comes along, and, as I remarked before, do not put in any more crops than can positively receive proper attention. The matter of marketing will require some judgment. Green crops will have to be sold when fit, let the prices be what they may, but dry roots have a season of four months, sometimes selling highest in the fall, at others late in the winter, and *vice versa*. As a rule, it is best to sell off the most of any crop when fair prices can be obtained.

SUGGESTIONS ON SEED GROWING.

The raising and cultivation of the plants, the harvesting and cleaning of the seeds and the manner of storing them are treated by Mr. Brill in a thoroughly practical manner. There are some points bearing upon successful seed-growing, omitted by him, which it is proposed to briefly present in this chapter.

The great majority of our vegetables are quite unlike the plant in its wild state. By cultivation through a long series of years, some part of the plant, that portion most useful to man, has taken on an unnatural development. This may occur in the root, as in the carrot; the tuber as in the potato; in the bulb as in the onion; in the stem as in kohl-rabi; in the leaves as in spinach; in the leaf-stalk as in rhubarb, or in the terminal bud, of which the cabbage is an example; the fruit is changed in a large number, as in the squashes, tomato, etc., and finally the seeds themselves are modified, as the peas, beans, sweet corn, etc. These portions have not only been increased in size, but they have acquired peculiar color, flavor, etc., which add to their value. When these plants are grown under unfavorable conditions, they revert more or less to their original wild state. The carrot affords a marked illustration of reversion. Allowed to sow its own seed in poor soil in autumn, the plant which comes up the following spring is left to fight its way among grass and other plants, and in a few years it becomes the well-known "wild carrot." The small woody root of this has been, by a few years of cultivation, brought back to the large tender root we know in the carrot. Many other examples could be cited of the tendency of cultivated plants to retrograde, but this is sufficient to show that the

FIRST POINT IN SEED-GROWING

is good cultivation of the plants which bear the seed. They must be kept from reverting towards their first condition; indeed, one of the methods of improving plants, and, consequently their seeds, is to provide those conditions which will allow them to assume their greatest development. In other words, high cultivation is necessary.

But comparatively little has been done in this country in the production of new varieties.

PRODUCTION OF NEW VARIETIES.

The few efforts in this direction have produced results which should encourage others to undertake the work. New varieties in vegetables are obtained mainly by two methods: by selection and by crossing.

The method of selection can be practised by every one. Indeed, selection is of the greatest importance in maintaining a variety at its present standard of excellence. All annual plants from which seeds are to be grown should have the operation of "rogueing" rigorously applied. When the plants are large enough to show their character, the bed should be carefully examined and every plant that does not come up to the standard fixed for that variety, pulled up and destroyed. We say that this is needed for annuals; it is equally required by biennials and perennials, but as these usually have to be taken up for the winter, selection can be made when they are handled for another purpose.

While plants raised from seed are much alike, so much so that we recognize them as belonging to the same variety, they are not absolutely alike, and sometimes the departures from the type are quite marked. By selecting such plants as show a tendency, be it ever so slight, in any desired direction, sowing the seed of these, selecting from the progeny the individuals to furnish seed for the next sowing, etc., a variety may be in time established. Thus the flat and the globe onions were obtained in this manner.

THE IMPORTANCE OF SELECTION

should be recognized by every seed-grower. While necessary if a variety is to be kept up to the standard, it must be applied rigorously by the seed-grower in raising his "stock seed." The seed-grower who cares for his reputation will send out seed from only well-grown and well-formed specimens, having rejected all others, but the selection for "stock seed"—that is, the seed he sows himself, is made with much greater care, endeavoring to insure uniformity in size, shape, color, etc. Upon care in selecting his stock seed much of the success of the seed-grower will depend.

When selection is followed for the purpose of obtaining and establishing a new variety, it is continued through a series of years, selecting with great care and severity, until the peculiarities aimed at are well fixed. It sometimes happens that a seedling strikingly unlike any of the others will be found in a bed. All such should be watched, and if they promise to be of value, be fairly tested.

WHEN VARIETIES ARE PRODUCED BY CROSSING

the characters of two distinct kinds are united and continued in one. As there are some intelligent persons who do not understand the arrangement of sexes in flowers, it will be necessary to briefly explain the parts and their relations to one another. Any of the lilies will answer for an example, as the parts are large and distinct. We have in the lily, as in most flowers, the corolla or showy part of the flower, which, in this, is composed of six parts. The greenish object seen in the very centre of the flower is the pistil. This at its base, down in the narrow part of the flower, has a large, oblong portion, the ovary. From this extends a long and slender stem, the style, at the top of which is a sort of knob, the stigma. Within the ovary, which in the lily has three divisions, each division contains numerous little bodies, the ovules, which in time will ripen into seeds. Other flowers may show a different arrangement. There may be several pistils, the ovary may have a different shape, and in some the style is much shorter or none at all, the stigma being directly upon the ovary. The ovary of the lily contains many ovules; others may have but few or even but one. The pistil is regarded as the female, its ovary, as in animals, containing ovules.

These ovules, whether few or many, do not grow and become seeds unless they are influenced by the male organs. These (the stamens), in the lily are six, and are arranged around the pistil; each has a slender stalk (filament) at the top of which is borne (and in this flower hung by the middle) a pouch or case, the anther, which, when ripe, opens by slits and lets out a yellow or brownish powder, the pollen. In other flowers the stamens may be fewer or more numerous, the anthers of different shape and not hung by the middle to the end of the filament, which may be much shorter or nearly absent. The office of the stamen is to produce pollen; this falls upon the stigma, which at the proper time is moist with a sticky liquid. Soon after the pollen touches the stigma, the ovules begin to grow and the ovary enlarges; in time it becomes the seed. When the pollen-grain touches the stigma it does not, as some have stated, drop down through an opening in the style, and thus reach the ovule. The pollen makes a growth; fine threads issue from it and passing down through the style, in time reach the ovules, which by this act are fertilized. An embryo is formed in them, they grow to the proper size, and are seeds. In the lily the stamens and pistil are in the same flower. The squash, cucumber, etc., have them in separate flowers, but on the same plant, while the beet has them in separate flowers which are on different plants. The ovules and ovaries can not grow unless they are fertilized by the pollen. Where the stamens and pistils are in separate flowers, whether they are on the same or on different plants, the pollen can not reach the stigma without aid. It is sometimes carried by the wind and very often by insects which, visiting the flowers in search of nectar, become dusted with the pollen, which they carry to the flowers with pistils; some of it gets rubbed upon the stigma and fertilization is effected. When the pollen of one variety of vegetable is placed upon the stigma of another variety, and a seed is formed, it is probable that the progeny of this seed will show the peculiarities of both varieties. The resulting vegetable will be a cross between the two.

CROSSES AND HYBRIDS.

These terms are often incorrectly used; they do not mean the same. A cross, as has been already explained, is produced between two varieties, while a hybrid results from fertilizing one species of plant with the pollen of another. Hybrids are much less frequent, and when produced are not apt to be fertile. Crosses are very frequently but incorrectly called hybrids. Crossing is an important means of obtaining new varieties. When the stamens and pistils are in separate flowers it is easily performed by applying the pollen to the stigma of the pistil of another variety, and covering the flower with muslin to keep off insects. When stamens and pistils are both in the same flower the task is more difficult. The anthers must be removed before they open, and the pollen applied as soon as the stigma is ready, which is known by the appearance of moisture on its surface. By judicious crossing valuable varieties have been obtained. Thus: the "American Wonder" pea is a cross between "Little Gem" and "Champion of England." The "Essex Hybrid" squash is a cross between the "Hubbard" and the "Turban." This method can only succeed in the hands of those who can handle small objects skillfully. Those who wish to practice it should make themselves familiar with the structure of the flowers upon which they propose to operate.

THE PRESERVATION OF POLLEN.

Pollen may be kept for days or weeks and still retain its vitality; indeed instances are known of its preservation for several months. It is usually preserved by wrapping it in a piece of tin-foil. When it is necessary to keep it for a very long time, it is placed in a glass tube which is carefully sealed up to exclude the air. Pollen is usually applied to the stigma of the flower to be fertilized by the aid of a small camel's-hair pencil.

In cross fertilizing, when both staminate and pistillate flowers are in proper condition at the same time, and the staminate are in abundance, the mere placing of the anthers in contact with the stigma will answer. This is a rather rough method of operating, but is effective under proper conditions.

Quite as important as any other step in cross-fertilizing is the covering of the flowers that have been operated on, in order to keep off insects which, by bringing pollen of the same variety, might interfere with the action of that of another variety that had already been applied.

The flowers, as soon as the pollen has been applied, should be surrounded by a piece of gauze, or similar material until the swelling of the ovary shows that fertilization has been effected.

While the crossing of one variety of a plant with another is of great utility when under proper control,

PROMISCUOUS CROSSING

may be a source of great loss to the seed-grower. It is a matter of common observation that nearly related varieties of vegetables, if grown near together, will intercross or, in popular language, will "mix." Crossing even when done intentionally, is not always attended by improvement in the progeny. It often happens that a plant which is the result of a cross, will inherit the bad qualities of both parents, and the usual effect of accidental crossing is to produce mongrels, inferior to either parent.

The readiness with which this takes place differs greatly. It is a matter of common observation that Indian corn, whether of field or sweet varieties, will "mix" with great readiness. In this plant the pollen is transported by the winds and crossing is often effected at great distances.

In the *Cucurbitaceæ*, the family to which the squash, melon, cucumber, etc., belong, the pollen is not carried by the wind, but the large and attractive flowers are abundantly visited by bees and other insects, which, while they do good service in fertilizing the female flowers, or, as gardeners say, in "setting the fruit," when their labors are confined to plants of the same variety, may do great injury in bringing pollen from other varieties. In raising seeds of plants of this family, this is a source of injury that should be kept in view and guarded against.

INJURY FROM CROSSING.

It is fortunate that the seeds of these plants retain their vitality longer than most others; indeed it is thought that they are improved by being kept a number of years before sowing them, the plants having less tendency to run to vine and being more fruitful. This fact allows the seed-grower to have but one variety of squash, etc. in bloom each year. In that year he can raise a sufficient quantity of seed to last several years, as it may be kept without deteriorating. A number of varieties of "ornamental gourds" are in cultivation; they are often grown as climbing vines, but especially for the fruit. This is usually not larger than a hen's egg, of various shapes, and marked and striped with several different colors. These gourds, or some of them at least, are varieties of *Colocynthis*, and have an intense bitterness like the medicinal colocynth. It is within the writer's knowledge that a crop of squashes was utterly ruined, the flesh being so bitter that it could not be eaten even by cattle. As ornamental gourds grew near-by, the flesh of which was intensely bitter, it is proper to infer that the bitterness of the squashes was due to the influence of their pollen. The danger is so great that the cultivation of the gourds should be abolished.

While these and other plants are noted for the readiness with which they cross, with others there is little or no danger. Different varieties of peas, for example, and of beans, may be grown in neighboring rows without admixture. While these flowers are visited by insects, it is probable that they are fertilized by their own pollen before they are sufficiently open to be attractive to bees and other insects. Grasses and the cereal grains, it is well known, are always fertilized before the parts of the flower open. Another source of danger to the seed-grower is in those plants which having escaped from cultivation, have become weeds, of which the carrot and parsnip are common examples. The pollen of these reverted plants seems to be more vigorous than that of the cultivated, and there is always danger that seed-bearing flowers of the carrot and parsnip may be fertilized by pollen from any wild plants that may be in the vicinity. From the readiness with which the wild radish may be improved and made to bear an edible root, there is reason to apprehend danger to radish seed if raised where the wild radish or charlock is a common weed.

THE VITALITY OF SEEDS.

Seeds vary greatly in the length of time for which they preserve their vitality. The seeds of some vegetables, the parsnip for example, are rarely good after they are a year old, the majority may be kept without injury from two to four years, while the melon, cucumber, squash, and most others of that family, will be good at the end of ten years. Other seeds seem to keep an indefinite length of time. It is said that at the *Jardin des Plantes* in Paris, the annual sowing of the sensitive plant (*Mimosa pudica*) has been made from the same bag of seed for the past eighty years.

It is often desirable to know the length of time a kind of seed will keep, and several tables have been published, one of which, prepared by a seedsman of experience, is here given.

A TABLE SHOWING THE AVERAGE VITALITY OF SEEDS OF DIFFERENT KINDS.

	Years.		Years.
Artichokes	5	Kale	5
Asparagus	4	Leek	2
Bean	6	Lettuce	5
Bean (kidney)	3	Melon	5
Beet	5	Onion	2
Broccoli	5	Okra	2
Cabbage	5	Pea	4
Carrot	4	Pumpkin	5
Cauliflower	5	Radish	5
Celery	7	Salsify	2
Corn	2	Spinach	5
Cucumber	5	Squash	5
Egg-plant	7	Tomato	5
Endive	9	Turnip	5

Such tables are only approximately accurate, as much

depends upon the manner in which seeds are kept, the climate, etc.

THE EFFECT OF DRYING.

A moist and warm climate is unfavorable, as are sudden great changes in temperature. That the length of time the seed is kept before sowing has an effect upon the plants produced from it, is shown by melons, etc., which from fresh seed are much more productive of vines and less so of fruit, than those which are several years old. That drying produces a marked effect is shown by the chestnut, walnut, and others, which if allowed to become perfectly dry will not germinate at all. In "ameliorating" (as the French call it), or bringing wild plants into cultivation, it is found that the mere keeping of the seeds out of the ground during the winter and sowing them in the spring, give plants greatly superior to those from seeds which were self-sown and had remained in the earth all winter.

HOW SEEDS SHOULD BE KEPT.

A dry airy room is the best place for keeping seeds, and they should not be in air-tight vessels. Cloth bags are on this account better than tighter packages.

Some of the works advise keeping peas, beans, etc., in jugs, tin cases, etc., in order to keep out the "bugs." This implies that the insect attacks the peas, etc., after they are harvested, which is by no means the case. The parent of both the pea-weevil and the bean-weevil, lays its eggs upon the outside of the young pod. The larva or maggot which hatches from these, makes its way to the growing seed which it enters and there lives and feeds. When it has made its growth, it becomes a pupa and remains dormant, usually until the seed is sown in the spring, though it sometimes comes out earlier. Whenever peas, etc., are found to be "buggy" the insects in the form of caterpillar or pupa, were within the seeds when they were harvested. When such seeds are placed in a close vessel and a little turpentine or benzine is added it will usually kill the insects. Bisulphide of carbon will most certainly do so.

THE INJURY CAUSED BY THE PEA WEEVIL.

From the fact that the weevil does not attack the germ, and that infested seed peas will germinate, it has been inferred that such peas were not injured, but as good as sound seed. This is a great error; while it is true that the insect does not destroy the germ, it robs it of its food. A sound pea has within it a sufficient supply of nutritive material to support the growth of the young plant until it can provide for itself by means of its roots. It is evident that if it is deprived of a large share of this, the germ will be poorly nourished. If the plant is starved at the outset, its whole after-life will show the effects of this treatment. While this would be properly inferred, it has been shown by experiment to be true, the yield from rows of equal length sown with sound and buggy peas, gave results most decidedly in favor of the former.

HOW TO GET RID OF THE WEEVILS.

The pea weevil has spread to such an extent that there are at present few localities exempt. It is more numerous in warm localities than in cold ones, and it was supposed that on this account Canada would be free from the pest. Our seed dealers have had their seed peas grown in Canada on the supposition that the insect had not reached that country. But it appears that the weevil is about as numerous in Canada as elsewhere, and that the superior quality of Canada seed is due to great care in garbling, or picking over the seed before sending it out.

It would not be difficult to exterminate the weevil in a

locality, if there could be united action among the cultivators. It does little good for one to attempt to get rid of the insect alone, as his neighbors will supply him with a sufficient number at blossoming time to stock his peas with "bugs."

Wherever the pea-growers of a locality will agree to abstain from raising the crop for a year, the insect may be suppressed. This need not deprive the people of the luxury of green peas, as the weevil can only come to perfection in the ripe seed.

The bean-weevil, which has become a serious evil only during the past dozen years, is still more destructive than that which attacks the pea; while there is but a single weevil in a pea, each bean may have several, sometimes a dozen or more. This, like the pea weevil, may be kept in check wherever the growers will act together for the purpose.

When there is the least doubt as to the freshness or vitality of seeds, they should be carefully tested before selling them or before sowing them. For sowing there may be a large enough share of the seed good to allow them to be used, if sown sufficiently thickly to make up for the loss, hence in testing seeds it is desirable to know just what proportion will germinate, and in

TESTING THE VITALITY OF SEEDS

the number should be carefully counted. In Germany an apparatus for testing seeds is employed, consisting of porous pottery which keeps the seeds continuously moist. The most satisfactory method of testing is that which surrounds the seeds as nearly as possible with the conditions they will meet with when sown. On this account the test of actual sowing is preferable to others. The close contact of the soil with the seed appears to influence germination, and the compacting or "firming" of the soil after sowing often makes the difference between failure and success. Those who have green-houses can make tests of seeds with great readiness; others will find the best substitute in a box of soil, such as is used for raising seedlings placed at the window of a kitchen or other constantly occupied room. Counting out fifty or one hundred seeds and sowing them in such a box will give the percentage that will be likely to grow when sown in field or garden. Another method is to fold up the counted seeds in a piece of cloth or blotting or other porous paper, and place them in the bottom of a small flower-pot. This pot is plunged in the soil of another pot two or more sizes larger; another pot, the size of the first, is filled with earth and placed within the second pot as a cover to the packet of seeds. The whole affair is set in the proper temperature and the earth kept moist. This is the next best method to sowing and has the advantage that it allows the process of germination to be watched, as the seeds may be readily examined from time to time.

Seeds which germinate readily, may be placed between folds of paper or cloth which is to be moistened, laid upon a dinner plate and covered by another; keeping this in a warm place with proper attention to moistening as required, will allow the proportion of good seed to be ascertained with sufficient accuracy.

From what has been said, it will be seen that seed-growing, while it is liable to losses and drawbacks, is one that allows of the exercise of acute observation, and one in which those most familiar with the laws of vegetable growth may most readily avoid or overcome the obstacles. It may be looked upon as one of the higher departments of practical horticulture, and as such presents attractions offered by scarcely any other kind of soil cultivation.

NUMBER OF PLANTS OR HILLS ON AN ACRE.

Ft. Ft.	Plants.	Ft. In. Ft. In.	Plants.
40 by 40	27	4 6 by 4 6	2,151
39 by 39	28	4 by 4	2,722
38 by 38	30	3 6 by 3 6	3,556
37 by 37	31	3 by 3	4,840
36 by 36	33	3 by 2 6	5,808
35 by 35	35	3 by 2	7,260
34 by 34	37	3 by 1 6	9,680
33 by 33	40	3 by 1	14,520
32 by 32	42	2 6 by 2 6	6,969
31 by 31	45	2 6 by 2	8,712
30 by 30	48	2 6 by 1 6	11,616
29 by 29	51	2 6 by 1	17,424
28 by 28	55	2 by 2	10,890
27 by 27	59	2 by 1 6	14,496
26 by 26	64	2 by 1 4	16,335
25 by 25	70	2 by 1 2	18,008
24 by 24	75	2 by 1	21,780
23 by 23	82	2 by 10	21,969
22 by 22	90	2 by 8	32,670
21 by 21	99	2 by 6	43,560
20 by 20	109	1 8 by 1 8	15,681
19 by 19	121	1 8 by 1 6	17,424
18 by 18	135	1 8 by 1 4	19,602
17 by 17	151	1 8 by 1 2	22,402
16 by 16	171	1 8 by 1	26,136
15 by 15	194	1 8 by 10	31,362
14 by 14	223	1 8 by 8	39,204
13 by 13	258	1 8 by 6	52,272
Ft. In. Ft. In.	Plants.	1 6 by 1 6	19,008
12 by 12	302	1 6 by 1 4	22,058
10 6 by 10 6	361	1 6 by 1 2	25,288
10 by 10	436	1 6 by 1	29,040
9 6 by 9 6	482	1 6 by 10	34,859
9 by 9	538	1 6 by 8	43,560
8 6 by 8 6	602	1 6 by 6	58,080
8 by 8	680	1 4 by 8	49,005
7 6 by 7 6	775	1 4 by 6	65,340
7 by 7	889	1 4 by 4	98,010
6 6 by 6 6	1,031	1 by 1	43,560
6 by 6	1,210	1 by 8	65,340
5 6 by 5 6	1,440	1 by 6	87,120
5 by 5	1,742	1 by 4	130,680

INDEX.

Asparagus 40
" Cutting and Bunching... 44
" Growing for Family Use. 45
" Growing Plants 40
" Planting and Cultivating 42
" Preparation and Soil for. 41
" Raising Seed of......... 45
" Varieties of........... 46
Beans, Bush or Dwarf.... 46
" Planting and Cultivating... 47
" Pole or Running............ 49
" Preparing for Market....... 47
" Raising Seed.............. 47
" Soil and Preparation for.. . 46
" Varieties of... 48
Beets.... 50
" Gathering and Storing...... 53
" Preparing for Market... 52
" Raising Seed.............. 53
" Soil and Preparation for...... 51
" Sowing and Cultivating...... 51
" Varieties of 56
Broccoli 57
Buildings 35
Cabbages, Early. 57
" Cutting and Marketing.. 60
" Planting and Cultivating 60
" Raising Seed 61
" Soil and Preparation for. 57
" Sowing Seed and Growing Plants. 58
" Varieties 63
Cabbages, Late 65
" Cutting and Marketing.. 68
" Planting and Cultivating. 67
" Raising Seed 68
" Soil and Preparation for. 65
" Sowing Seed and Growing Plants 66
" Storing for Winter 68
" Varieties 71
Cabbage, Turnip-Rooted 72
Carrots 75
" Gathering and Storing..... 77
" Preparing for Market 76
" Raising Seed 77
" Soil and Preparation... ... 75
" Sowing and Cultivating ... 75
" Varieties of... 78
Cauliflower 72
" Marketing 74
" Raising Seed.. 74
" Soil and Preparation for. 73
" Varieties............... 75

Celery 79
" Planting and Cultivating.... 80
" Preparing for Market........ 82
" Raising Seed.... 84
" Soil and Preparation... 79
" Sowing Seed and Growing Plants.................... 80
" Storing for Market.......... 84
" Varieties of...... 85
Cold-Frames 22
Conclusion....... 149
Corn 86
" Marketing...... 87
" Raising Seed 88
" Soil and Preparation for... .. 86
" Varieties of................. 88
Cucumbers.... 89
" Marketing.... 91
" Raising Seed......... .. 92
" Planting and Cultivating 89
" Varieties of............ . 93
Egg-Plants........ 94
" Cutting for Market...... 97
" Raising Seed.......... 97
" Soil, Planting and Cultivation....... 96
" Sowing Seed and Growing Plants... 94
" Varieties of............. 99
Forcing-Pit. 27
Gardening, Farm.................. 8
" Market 7
General Management. 149
Herbs.. 100
Horseradish... 102
" Gathering and Storing.104
" Planting and Cultivation of.... 103
" Preparing for Market..104
" Soil and Preparation for... 103
Hot-Beds.... 25
Implements, Cultivator............ 29
" Dibble.............. 31
" Forks 32
" Garden-Line... 30
" Harrow............. 28
" Hoe................ 29
" Markers............ 30
" Plow............... 28
" Rake............... 30
" Shears............. 32
" Spade.. 29
" Trowel.. 32

INDEX.

Insects............................ 19
Introduction...................... 5
Kale 105
Kohl-Rabi 72
Leeks.............................106
" Planting and Cultivation of. 107
" Preparing for Market........108
" Soil and Preparation for.....107
" Sowing Seed and Growing
    Plants 107
" Varieties of..................108
Lettuce...........................108
" Forcing 110
" Marketing....................111
" Planting and Cultivation..109
" Raising Seed..................111
" Soil and Preparation for....109
" Sowing Seed and Growing
    Plants 108
" Varieties of..................112
Machines, Fan-Mill................ 34
"   Seed-Sowers............... 31
"   Wagons.................... 35
"   Wheelbarrows............. 34
Manures and Manuring............. 12
Mats, Straw 32
Melons, Musk.....................113
"   Gathering for Market......114
"   Raising Seed..............114
"   Soil and Preparation for..113
"   Varieties of..............114
Melons, Water....................115
"   Gathering for Market......115
"   Raising Seed..............116
"   Soil and Preparation for..115
"   Varieties of..............116
Number of Plants or Hills on an
    Acre.........................151
Okra..............................117
" Cultivation of................118
" Cutting for Market............118
" Raising Seed..................118
" Varieties of..................118
Onions............................118
" Growing Sets..................122
" Preparing for Market.........122
" Raising Seed..................123
" Varieties of..................124
Parsley...........................125
" Raising Seed..................126
" Varieties of..................126
Parsnips..........................126
" Soil and Preparation for....127
" Varieties of..................127
Peas..............................128
" Marketing 129
" Raising Seed..................129
" Soil and Preparation for.....128
" Sowing and Cultivation.......128
" Varieties of..................130
Peppers...........................130
" Marketing.....................131
" Raising Seed..................131
" Varieties of..................131
Plowing, Fall..................... 38

Potatoes..........................131
"   Soil, Preparation, and
        Planting.................132
"   Varieties of..............134
Radishes..........................134
"   Marketing.................135
"   Raising Seed..............136
"   Soil, Preparation, and
        Sowing...................135
"   Varieties of..............137
Rhubarb 137
"   Marketing.................138
"   Raising Seed..............138
"   Soil and Planting.........137
"   Varieties of..............138
Roots, Storing for Winter........ 36
Sage..............................100
Salsify or Oyster-Plant..........138
"   Marketing.................138
"   Raising Seed..............139
"   Soil and Preparation for..138
Sashes............................ 33
Seed Cloths...................... 34
"   Growing................10, 155
"   Harvesting and Cleaning... 37
"   Sowing.................... 16
Shutters.......................... 34
Sieves............................ 34
Soil and Preparation............. 11
Spinach...........................137
"   Marketing.................140
"   Raising Seed..............140
"   Soil and Preparation for..139
"   Varieties of..............140
Squashes..........................141
"   Marketing.................141
"   Raising Seed..............141
"   Soil, Planting, etc., of .. 141
"   Varieties of..............142
Summer Savory....................101
Sweet Marjoram 101
Sweet Potatoes...................142
"   " Growing the Plants 142
"   " Marketing..........143
"   " Soil, Preparation, and
            Planting.............143
"   " Varieties of........144
Thyme.............................101
Tomatoes..........................144
"   Growing Plants............144
"   Marketing.................145
"   Raising Seed..............145
"   Soil, Preparation, and
        Planting.................144
"   Varieties of..............145
Tools and their Uses............. 28
Transplanting.................... 17
Turnips...........................146
"   Harvesting and Storing... 148
"   Marketing.................147
"   Raising Seed..............148
"   Soil and Preparation......146
"   Sowing and Cultivation...147
"   Varieties of..............148
Vegetables and their Seeds....... 40

STANDARD BOOKS.

Commended by the Greatest Educators of Germany, England and the United States. Endorsed by Officials, and adopted in many Schools

New Methods in Education

Art, Real Manual Training, Nature Study. Explaining Processes whereby Hand, Eye and Mind are Educated by Means that Conserve Vitality and Develop a Union of Thought and Action

By J. Liberty Tadd

Director of the Public School of Industrial Art, of Manual Training and Art in the R. C. High School, and in several Night Schools, Member of the Art Club, Sketch Club, and Educational Club, and of the Academy of Natural Sciences, Philadelphia

BASED on twenty-two years' experience with thousands of children and hundreds of teachers. "A method reasonable, feasible and without great cost, adapted to all grades, from child to adult; a plan that can be applied without friction to every kind of educational institution or to the family, and limited only by the capacity of the individual; a method covered by natural law, working with the absolute precision of nature itself; a process that unfolds the capacities of children as unfold the leaves and flowers; a system that teaches the pupils that they are in the plan and part of life, and enables them to work out their own salvation on the true lines of design and work as illustrated in every natural thing."

A Wealth of Illustration—478 Pictures and 44 Full-Page Plates

showing children and teachers practicing these new methods or their work. A revelation to all interested in developing the wonderful capabilities of young or old. The pictures instantly fascinate every child, imbuing it with a desire to do likewise. Teachers and parents at once become enthusiastic and delighted over the Tadd methods which this book enables them to put into practice. Not a hackneyed thought nor a stale picture. Fresh, new, practical, scientific, inspiring

AMONG THOSE WHO ENDORSE THE WORK ARE

HERBERT SPENCER, DR. W. W. KEENE, PRESIDENT HUEY—Of the Philadelphia board of education.
SECRETARY GOTZE—Of the leading pedagogical society of Germany (by which the book is being translated into German for publication at Berlin).
CHARLES H. THURBER—Professor of Pedagogy, University of Chicago.
TALCOTT WILLIAMS—Editor Philadelphia Press, Book News, etc.
R. H. WEBSTER—Superintendent of Schools, San Francisco.
DR. A. E. WINSHIP—Editor Journal of Education.
W. F. SLOCUM—President Colorado College.
FREDERICK WINSOR—Head master The Country School for Boys of Baltimore City, under the auspices of Johns Hopkins University.
G. B. MORRISON—Principal Manual Training High School, Kansas City.
DR. EDWARD KIRK—Dean University of Penn.
G. E. DAWSON—(Clark University), Professor of Psychology, Bible Normal College.
ROMAN STEINER—Baltimore.

SPECIFICATIONS: Size, 7½x10½ inches, almost a quarto; 458 pages, fine plate paper, beautifully bound in cloth and boards, cover illuminated in gold; weight, 4½ lbs. Boxed, price $3.00 net, postpaid to any part of the world.

Orange Judd Company

New York, N. Y., 52-54 Lafayette Place. Springfield, Mass., Homestead Bg Chicago, Ill., Marquette Building.

SENT FREE ON APPLICATION

Descriptive Catalog of---

Containing 100 8vo. pages, profusely illustrated, and giving full descriptions of the best works on the following subjects:

RURAL BOOKS

Farm and Garden
Fruits, Flowers, Etc.
Cattle, Sheep and Swine
Dogs, Horses, Riding, Etc.
Poultry, Pigeons and Bees
Angling and Fishing
Boating, Canoeing and Sailing
Field Sports and Natural History
Hunting, Shooting, Etc.
Architecture and Building
Landscape Gardening
Household and Miscellaneous

Publishers and Importers

Orange Judd Company

52 and 54 Lafayette Place
NEW YORK

BOOKS WILL BE FORWARDED, POSTPAID, ON RECEIPT OF PRICE

Greenhouse Construction.

By Prof. L. R. Taft. A complete treatise on greenhouse structures and arrangements of the various forms and styles of plant houses for professional florists as well as amateurs. All the best and most approved structures are so fully and clearly described that anyone who desires to build a greenhouse will have no difficulty in determining the kind best suited to his purpose. The modern and most successful methods of heating and ventilating are fully treated upon. Special chapters are devoted to houses used for the growing of one kind of plants exclusively. The construction of hotbeds and frames receives appropriate attention. Over one hundred excellent illustrations, specially engraved for this work, make every point clear to the reader and add considerably to the artistic appearance of the book. Cloth, 12mo. $1.50

Greenhouse Management.

By L. R. Taft. This book forms an almost indispensable companion volume to Greenhouse Construction. In it the author gives the results of his many years' experience, together with that of the most successful florists and gardeners, in the management of growing plants under glass. So minute and practical are the various systems and methods of growing and forcing roses, violets, carnations, and all the most important florists' plants, as well as fruits and vegetables described, that by a careful study of this work and the following of its teachings, failure is almost impossible. Illustrated. Cloth, 12mo. $1.50

Bulbs and Tuberous-Rooted Plants.

By C. L. Allen. A complete treatise on the history, description, methods of propagation and full directions for the successful culture of bulbs in the garden, dwelling and greenhouse. As generally treated, bulbs are an expensive luxury, while when properly managed, they afford the greatest amount of pleasure at the least cost. The author of this book has for many years made bulb growing a specialty, and is a recognized authority on their cultivation and management. The illustrations which embellish this work have been drawn from nature, and have been engraved especially for this book. The cultural directions are plainly stated, practical and to the point. Cloth, 12mo. $1.50

Irrigation Farming.

By Lute Wilcox. A handbook for the practical application of water in the production of crops. A complete treatise on water supply, canal construction, reservoirs and ponds, pipes for irrigation purposes, flumes and their structure, methods of applying water, irrigation of field crops, the garden, the orchard and vineyard; windmills and pumps, appliances and contrivances. Profusely, handsomely illustrated. Cloth, 12mo.   . . $1.50

STANDARD BOOKS.

Landscape Gardening.

By F. A. Waugh, professor of horticulture, University of Vermont. A treatise on the general principles governing outdoor art; with sundry suggestions for their application in the commoner problems of gardening. Every paragraph is short, terse and to the point, giving perfect clearness to the discussions at all points. In spite of the natural difficulty of presenting abstract principles the whole matter is made entirely plain even to the inexperienced reader. Illustrated, 12mo. Cloth. . $.50

Fungi and Fungicides.

By Prof. Clarence M. Weed. A practical manual concerning the fungous diseases of cultivated plants and the means of preventing their ravages. The author has endeavored to give such a concise account of the most important facts relating to these as will enable the cultivator to combat them intelligently. 222 pp., 90 ill., 12mo. Paper, 50 cents; cloth. $1.00

Talks on Manure.

By Joseph Harris, M. S. A series of familiar and practical talks between the author and the deacon, the doctor, and other neighbors, on the whole subject of manures and fertilizers; including a chapter especially written for it by Sir John Bennet Lawes of Rothamsted, England. Cloth, 12mo. $1.50

Insects and Insecticides.

By Clarence M. Weed, D. Sc., Prof. of entomology and zoology, New Hampshire college of agriculture. A practical manual concerning noxious insects, and methods of preventing their injuries. 334 pages, with many illustrations. Cloth, 12mo. $1.50

Mushrooms. How to Grow Them.

By Wm. Falconer. This is the most practical work on the subject ever written, and the only book on growing mushrooms published in America. The author describes how he grows mushrooms, and how they are grown for profit by the leading market gardeners, and for home use by the most successful private growers. Engravings drawn from nature expressly for this work. Cloth. $1.00

Handbook of Plants and General Horticulture.

By Peter Henderson. This new edition comprises about 50 per cent. more genera than the former one, and embraces the botanical name, derivation, natural order, etc., together with a short history of the different genera, concise instructions for their propagation and culture, and all the leading local or common English names, together with a comprehensive glossary of botanical and technical terms. Plain instructions are also given for the cultivation of the principal vegetables, fruits and flowers. Cloth, large 8vo. $3.00

Ginseng, Its Cultivation, Harvesting, Marketing and Market Value.

By Maurice G. Kains, with a short account of its history and botany. It discusses in a practical way how to begin with either seed or roots, soil, climate and location, preparation, planting and maintenance of the beds, artificial propagation, manures, enemies, selection for market and for improvement, preparation for sale, and the profits that may be expected. This booklet is concisely written, well and profusely illustrated, and should be in the hands of all who expect to grow this drug to supply the export trade, and to add a new and profitable industry to their farms and gardens, without interfering with the regular work. 12mo. . . . . . $.35

Land Draining.

A handbook for farmers on the principles and practice of draining, by Manly Miles, giving the results of his extended experience in laying tile drains. The directions for the laying out and the construction of tile drains will enable the farmer to avoid the errors of imperfect construction, and the disappointment that must necessarily follow. This manual for practical farmers will also be found convenient for references in regard to many questions that may arise in crop growing, aside from the special subjects of drainage of which it treats. Cloth, 12mo. $1.00

Henderson's Practical Floriculture.

By Peter Henderson. A guide to the successful propagation and cultivation of florists' plants. The work is not one for florists and gardeners only, but the amateur's wants are constantly kept in mind, and we have a very complete treatise on the cultivation of flowers under glass, or in the open air, suited to those who grow flowers for pleasure as well as those who make them a matter of trade. Beautifully illustrated. New and enlarged edition. Cloth, 12mo. $1.50

Tobacco Leaf.

By J. B. Killebrew and Herbert Myrick. Its Culture and Cure, Marketing and Manufacture. A practical handbook on the most approved methods in growing, harvesting, curing, packing, and selling tobacco, with an account of the operations in every department of tobacco manufacture. The contents of this book are based on actual experiments in field, curing barn, packing house, factory and laboratory. It is the only work of the kind in existence, and is destined to be the standard practical and scientific authority on the whole subject of tobacco for many years. Upwards of 500 pages and 150 original engravings. $2.00

STANDARD BOOKS.

Play and Profit in My Garden.

By E. P. Roe. The author takes us to his garden on the rocky hillsides in the vicinity of West Point, and shows us how out of it, after four years' experience, he evoked a profit of $1,000, and this while carrying on pastoral and literary labor. It is very rarely that so much literary taste and skill are mated to so much agricultural experience and good sense. Cloth, 12mo. . . $1.00

Forest Planting.

By H. Nicholas Jarchow, LL. D. A treatise on the care of woodlands and the restoration of the denuded timberlands on plains and mountains. The author has fully described those European methods which have proved to be most useful in maintaining the superb forests of the old world. This experience has been adapted to the different climates and trees of America, full instructions being given for forest planting of our various kinds of soil and subsoil, whether on mountain or valley. Illustrated, 12mo. $1.50

Soils and Crops of the Farm.

By George E. Morrow, M. A., and Thomas F. Hunt. The methods of making available the plant food in the soil are described in popular language. A short history of each of the farm crops is accompanied by a discussion of its culture. The useful discoveries of science are explained as applied in the most approved methods of culture. Illustrated. Cloth, 12mo. $1.00

American Fruit Culturist.

By John J. Thomas. Containing practical directions for the propagation and culture of all the fruits adapted to the United States. Twentieth thoroughly revised and greatly enlarged edition by Wm. H. S. Wood. This new edition makes the work practically almost a new book, containing everything pertaining to large and small fruits as well as sub-tropical and tropical fruits. Richly illustrated by nearly 800 engravings. 758 pp., 12mo. $2.50

Fertilizers.

By Edward B. Voorhees, director of the New Jersey Agricultural Experiment Station. It has been the aim of the author to point out the underlying principles and to discuss the important subjects connected with the use of fertilizer materials. The natural fertility of the soil, the functions of manures and fertilizers, and the need of artificial fertilizers are exhaustively discussed. Separate chapters are devoted to the various fertilizing elements, to the purchase, chemical analyses, methods of using fertilizers, and the best fertilizers for each of the most important field, garden and orchard crops. 335 pp. $1.00

Gardening for Profit.

By Peter Henderson. The standard work on market and family gardening. The successful experience of the author for more than thirty years, and his willingness to tell, as he does in this work, the secret of his success for the benefit of others, enables him to give most valuable information. The book is profusely illustrated. Cloth, 12mo. $1.50

Herbert's Hints to Horse Keepers.

By the late Henry William Herbert (Frank Forester). This is one of the best and most popular works on the horse prepared in this country. A complete manual for horsemen, embracing: How to breed a horse; how to buy a horse; how to break a horse; how to use a horse; how to feed a horse; how to physic a horse (allopathy or homoeopathy); how to groom a horse; how to drive a horse; how to ride a horse, etc. Beautifully illustrated. Cloth, 12mo. $1.50

Barn Plans and Outbuildings.

Two hundred and fifty-seven illustrations. A most valuable work, full of ideas, hints, suggestions, plans, etc., for the construction of barns and outbuildings, by practical writers. Chapters are devoted to the economic erection and use of barns, grain barns, house barns, cattle barns, sheep barns, corn houses, smoke houses, ice houses, pig pens, granaries, etc. There are likewise chapters on bird houses, dog houses, tool sheds, ventilators, roofs and roofing, doors and fastenings, workshops, poultry houses, manure sheds, barnyards, root pits, etc, Cloth, 12mo. $1.00

Cranberry Culture.

By Joseph J. White. Contents: Natural history, history of cultivation, choice of location, preparing the ground, planting the vines, management of meadows, flooding, enemies and difficulties overcome, picking, keeping, profit and loss. Cloth, 12mo. $1.00

Ornamental Gardening for Americans.

By Elias A. Long, landscape architect. A treatise on beautifying homes, rural districts and cemeteries. A plain and practical work with numerous illustrations and instructions so plain that they may be readily followed. Illustrated. Cloth, 12mo. $1.50

Grape Culturist.

By A. S. Fuller. This is one of the very best of works on the culture of the hardy grapes, with full directions for all departments of propagation, culture, etc., with 150 excellent engravings, illustrating planting, training, grafting, etc. Cloth, 12mo. $1.50

STANDARD BOOKS.

Turkeys and How to Grow Them.

Edited by Herbert Myrick. A treatise on the natural history and origin of the name of turkeys; the various breeds, the best methods to insure success in the business of turkey growing. With essays from practical turkey growers in different parts of the United States and Canada. Copiously illustrated. Cloth, 12mo. . . $1.00

Profits I Poultry.

Useful and ornamental breeds and their profitable management. This excellent work contains the combined experience of a number of practical men in all departments of poultry raising. It is profusely illustrated and forms a unique and important addition to our poultry literature. Cloth, 12mo. $1.00

How Crops Grow.

By Prof. Samuel W. Johnson of Yale College. New and revised edition. A treatise on the chemical composition, structure and life of the plant. This book is a guide to the knowledge of agricultural plants, their composition, their structure and modes of development and growth; of the complex organization of plants, and the use of the parts; the germination of seeds, and the food of plants obtained both from the air and the soil. The book is indispensable to all real students of agriculture. With numerous illustrations and tables of analysis. Cloth, 12mo. $1.50

Coburn's Swine Husbandry.

By F. D. Coburn. New, revised and enlarged edition. The breeding, rearing, and management of swine, and the prevention and treatment of their diseases. It is the fullest and freshest compendium relating to swine breeding yet offered. Cloth, 12mo. $1.50

Stewart's Shepherd's Manual.

By Henry Stewart. A valuable practical treatise on the sheep for American farmers and sheep growers. It is so plain that a farmer or a farmer's son who has never kept a sheep, may learn from its pages how to manage a flock successfully, and yet so complete that even the experienced shepherd may gather many suggestions from it. The results of personal experience of some years with the characters of the various modern breeds of sheep, and the sheep raising capabilities of many portions of our extensive territory and that of Canada—and the careful study of the diseases to which our sheep are chiefly subject, with those by which they may eventually be afflicted through unforeseen accidents—as well as the methods of management called for under our circumstances, are carefully described. Illustrated. Cloth, 12mo. $1.00

STANDARD BOOKS.

Feeds and Feeding.

By W. A. Henry. This handbook for students and stock men constitutes a compendium of practical and useful knowledge on plant growth and animal nutrition, feeding stuffs, feeding animals and every detail pertaining to this important subject. It is thorough, accurate and reliable, and is the most valuable contribution to live stock literature in many years. All the latest and best information is clearly and systematically presented, making the work indispensable to every owner of live stock. 658 pages, 8vo. Cloth. $2.00

Hunter and Trapper.

By Halsey Thrasher, an old and experienced sportsman. The best modes of hunting and trapping are fully explained, and foxes, deer, bears, etc., fall into his traps readily by following his directions. Cloth, 12mo. $ .50

The Ice Crop.

By Theron L. Hiles. How to harvest, ship and use ice. A complete, practical treatise for farmers, dairymen, ice dealers, produce shippers, meat packers, cold storers, and all interested in ice houses, cold storage, and the handling or use of ice in any way. Including many recipes for iced dishes and beverages. The book is illustrated by cuts of the tools and machinery used in cutting and storing ice, and the different forms of ice houses and cold storage buildings. 122 pp., ill., 16mo. Cloth. $1.00

Practical Forestry.

By Andrew S. Fuller. A treatise on the propagation, planting and cultivation, with descriptions and the botanical and popular names of all the indigenous trees of the United States, and notes on a large number of the most valuable exotic species. $1.50

Irrigation for the Farm, Garden and Orchard.

By Henry Stewart. This work is offered to those American farmers and other cultivators of the soil who, from painful experience, can readily appreciate the losses which result from the scarcity of water at critical periods. Fully illustrated. Cloth, 12mo. $1.00

Market Gardening and Farm Notes.

By Burnett Landreth. Experiences and observation for both North and South, of interest to the amateur gardener, trucker and farmer. A novel feature of the book is the calendar of farm and garden operations for each month of the year; the chapters on fertilizers, transplanting, succession and rotation of crops, the packing, shipping and marketing of vegetables will be especially useful to market gardeners. Cloth, 12mo. . . $1.00

This book is a preservation facsimile.
It is made in compliance with copyright law
and produced on acid-free archival
60# book weight paper
which meets the requirements of
ANSI/NISO Z39.48-1992 (permanence of paper)

Preservation facsimile printing and binding
by
Acme Bookbinding
Charlestown, Massachusetts

2006

www.ingramcontent.com/pod-product-compliance
Lightning Source LLC
Chambersburg PA
CBHW032154160426
43197CB00008B/910